# Pillar
of
# Stone

## Words that changed my life forever

*Gloria Bernard*

# PILLAR OF STONE

## "Words that Changed My Life Forever"

## BY GLORIA BERNARD

Kravitz & Sons
INNOVATORS IN PUBLISHING, MARKETING AND ADVERTISING

**Kravitz and Sons LLC**
1301 Farmville Blvd, Suite 104
Greenville, NC 27834

Published by Kravitz and Sons LLC.

 ISBN:    979-8-89639-295-8  (sc)
 ISBN:    979-8-89639-296-5  (e)

Library of Congress Control Number: 2025916836

# Author's Note

This is only a small glimpse into my life. I am attempting to share just a few of the bizarre and dysfunctional events of my life, some that happened as a child and some as an adult, as I remember them today. I grew up with an abusive and alcoholic father, a mother who suffered from schizophrenia, and a sister who took care of me when we were young. My sister disowned me for over twenty years, then briefly came back into my life only to disown me again. Both my parents are deceased, and my sister still wants nothing to do with me.

I wrote this book off and on for over twenty years. I would pull it out and work on it for a while then put it aside for another time in my life when I was ready to reflect and write. Not every detail is completely accurate, but it is to the best of my memory. Names have been changed so as not to offend anyone or anyone's family.

At times, writing my story was cleansing and fun; at other times—when I found myself filled with emotion, sometimes sad and sometimes happy—it was difficult. Overall, writing this book was a very gratifying experience.

# To Marcellus and Crystal

This book was written for and now dedicated to my two children, Marcellus, and Crystal. They have been the focal point of my life. They have brought me so much joy and laughter, and I love them both so much and am incredibly proud as well. May they find a better understanding of their mother by reading this book and know why I do and say the things they don't always understand. May they find the inner strength that I know they have to move through their life with passion and joy despite the setbacks or obstacles they will surely experience. Most important may they learn the true meaning of "Happiness" and learn to combat the inner demons by reducing anxiety and self-doubt and increasing inner peace. May they learn to focus on the now and be present as much as possible while planning for the future. May they not dwell on the past, not listen to negative self-talk, not blame others, and just love themselves wheresoever they are at any particular time in their life.

Happiness is a choice. Happiness is the choice I made in spite of all the complex obstacles I had to overcome. May they always choose happiness.

# CONTENTS

# I
## Pillar of Stone

"Don't look back or you'll turn into a pillar of stone." Simple words spoken by my mother, but they changed my life forever. I was only four years old when I heard those words, I knew this was what it feels like to truly be all alone. I shuttered. I wanted to cry out, to scream for someone to help me, but no words formed in my mouth. I was too frightened to speak. I was screaming in silence. My mother, sitting in the front passenger seat of our family car, looking straight ahead, spoke these words to my sister and me. Florence and I were sitting in the back seat, and our dad was driving our old and run-down car. He said nothing, just kept driving down the long driveway from our house toward the main road, away from home, away from the security I used to feel and would never feel again. I looked over at my sister. She seemed so much older to me, and I always looked up to her for comfort and guidance. Her eyes were glued to the back of the front seat. She didn't move; she stared straight ahead. I sat there thinking *I want to look back, but I don't want to get into trouble for disobeying my mother. If I look back at our front yard to see all our personal belongings burning up in the huge pile, what will happen?* The huge pile my father and mother had just finished building, the pile I wanted to see but didn't want to get punished for looking at. Then I thought, if I turn into a pillar of stone, she can't hurt me, and then I will know for sure that my mother and perhaps my father are "crazy." Crazy was the only word that came to my mind. *This is crazy.* What my parents just spent all morning doing was crazy; therefore, they must be crazy. More importantly, I thought, if I look back and don't turn into a pillar of stone, I'll know that I'm *not* crazy. Do I look back or not? I'm thinking and pondering in my four-year-old mind. *If I turn into a pillar of stone, my mother will know that I disobeyed her, and I'll be in trouble. However, if I'm a pillar of stone, she can't spank me for disobeying. I'm going to do it.* I looked over at my sister. She was still looking straight ahead. I wondered, what was she thinking.

I was too afraid to ask her, and I didn't think she would tell me anyway. I took a deep breath. This could be my last, I thought. I ever so quietly lifted myself up in the seat and glanced at my sister again as I turned to sneak a peek out the high back window. She just stared at me with wide eyes and didn't say a word. I saw it! The fire! The huge pile made of all our belongings, burning fiercely. Everything that we owned, everything, was piled up high in our front yard, on fire. All our clothes, toys, furniture, dishes, pots, and pans, even all our food from the cupboards and refrigerator were burning up in the pile on the front yard. I stared at the fire for a minute thinking about my doll that my mother took from me just before she told me to get into the car. I had protested. "No, not my baby doll." My mother replied that God had told her that we had to burn everything we owned, "All our worldly possessions except the clothes we are wearing must be burned," she said. She removed the doll, which I was holding tightly in my arms, and threw it on the burning pile. I thought, *my God would not want me to burn my baby doll; this is wrong.*

I turned around and sat back in my seat and stared straight ahead. My doll was burning along with everything else. I looked over at my sister again. She turned her head and looked at me with a very frightened expression on her face. I wondered again what she was thinking, but I couldn't speak, and I don't think she could either. I must have been in shock. I looked straight ahead again as fright filled me up. I waited a short time. Nothing happened. I stared at my hands, arms, and legs. Well, I thought, *I won't get into trouble for turning around since I didn't turn into a pillar of stone. My mother won't know that I looked around. I'm still flesh and blood.* The fright I felt minutes ago suddenly changed and became so much more intense I could hardly breathe. I began to tremble. I just realized I was the only one in the car, the only one in my family who knew the truth. What my parents had just done was not normal, and now I loudly screamed the question inside my mind over and over as I sat there trembling. *I'm just a little girl; who is going to take care of me? My mother can't; she keeps saying things that don't make sense, and she keeps talking to someone who is not there. My father can't because he is going along with what my mother says. My sister can't. Even though she seems so much bigger than me, she's just a little girl too; besides, she didn't turn around to look, and that must mean she believes our mom and dad are right. No, I'm now all alone.* All alone with nothing, no one to comfort me, and nothing to hold on to, not even my doll that so many times before had brought me feelings of comfort. I keep thinking, *who's going to take care of me, who's going to take care of me,* over and over in desperation. Then, as the tears began to stream down my face, I heard a very gentle soothing voice from somewhere say, "Don't worry, I'll take care of you." I didn't know where the voice came from, but I heard it as clear as could be. I began to feel comforted. I had a feeling of warmth and caring come over me, and I stopped crying. I continued to stare at the back of the front seat until eventually, the humming of the car motor and the gentle bumping movement of the car put me to sleep.

That moment, my life changed forever. I now had to take on worries meant only for adults. The innocent little girl who used to know, without question, her mom and dad would take care of her could no longer depend on them, could no longer count on them to always be there for her. I had to be strong to survive. I began to think, *what if Mom says God is telling her that she should get rid of me and my sister?* I was afraid for my life. My only comfort was the soft voice that said, "Don't worry, I'll take care of you."

What happened? When I was much younger, I remember my father as a happy man.

He was always laughing, always playing prank tricks on me and my sister and my mother. My father's name is Chester, but his friends called him Chet and his family nickname was Bud. Mostly, my father worked in the logging industry in various places in Oregon and Northern California. I don't remember him being home very much, but he was usually playing games with my sister and me when he was home. The game we liked the most was Hide and Seek. The three of us would play it for hours. His work was not very stable, and we moved around often. My mother didn't work outside the home, and I remember her always doing something around the house. She was busy cleaning. She never had time to play with my sister or me. When we said, "Mom, come play with us," she would answer, "I will as soon as I finish this work." When the task was finished, she was busy doing something else.

What I didn't know then was that my mother was the oldest of seven brothers and sisters, and she didn't know how to play. She always had to help take care of her siblings or do chores around the house for her mother. My mother and her family are Spanish, and their home was in Albuquerque, New Mexico. My mother said our ancestors were from Spain. Castilian Spaniards, she would say. There was a time before I was the age of four, I remember living in a place very warm and sunny. We had a big yard and a garden area with a neighboring field that extended further than I could see. I remember walking with my mother and sister through that field to visit the neighboring house. The neighbor's house was nicer than ours, and she always had something good to eat.

The most fun I had while living there was taking care of a brood of baby ducks. My father put them in a large box in the house at night when they were young and would take them outside during the day. My sister and I would spend hours playing with them and watching them swim around the small pond in our yard. Eventually, they grew up and no longer needed to be kept in the house at night.

The worst memory I have of living in the house in this warm place is having my tonsils removed. My sister and I had them removed at the same time. Mine didn't need to be removed, but it was decided to remove mine at the same time. I was upset about this. I didn't think it was fair. My sister and I were in the same room in the hospital, and that gave me comfort, but I remember being very frightened. When we got home, our mother fixed our bed up in the living room by the large window. We would lie in bed looking out the window or color in our coloring books and eat pudding and ice cream. I soon forgot how frightened I was in the hospital.

I later learned the house was in Albuquerque, New Mexico, near to my grandmother's house. I was too young to remember her during this period. We did not stay there long. My father was out of work and decided we should move to Oregon, where he thought he could find work in the logging industry.

We moved to a house in Oregon. It could have been in northern California. Since we moved around often when I was young and never stayed in one place long my memory fails me on exactly where the homes were located. Sometimes we moved two and three times in one year. My sister started kindergarten not too long after we moved to a different house, and I was lonely and missed her during the day. I had no one to play with. My father soon lost his job, which happened yearly, and he began to play school with me for an hour or so every morning after my sister left for school. My dad was the teacher, and I was the student. He set up school in the living room, and the coffee table became my desk. My mother was busy with housework while my dad taught me to read and write. He taught me to say my ABCs, to print my name and a couple of other words, and he taught me to read. He also taught me how to add and subtract small numbers. I was so happy during that time. I loved playing school; I loved spending time with my dad. I wasn't lonely anymore. My mother got involved too by teaching me Spanish words. It was so much fun learning all these new things. I remember thinking, *if this is what school is like, I'm looking forward to going there.* I wasn't lonely anymore while my sister was in school, and I had something new to share with her when she got home.

A sad memory I have of living in this house was the night my mother was cutting kindling for the wood cook-stove, and she chopped her finger off. She was in pain. She was on the back porch cutting kindling; my father, sister and I were in the living room. I heard her moan as she came walking in with blood dripping everywhere. I was so scared. The three of us drove Mom to the hospital. I remember worrying about her dying. It was terrifying. As it turned out, they were able to save her finger, but it was never the same, and it bothered her from time to time for years.

We moved from that house and ended up living up in the woods near a small logging town in Oregon. My sister was in school, my father was working as a lumberjack or in a logging mill. I'm not sure which. Sometimes he worked in the woods as a choker setter. This meant he hooked the large clamps onto the logs that were then hauled away to the waiting log trucks. The choker was fastened to long cables attached to a crane. He loved being out in the woods even though the work was extremely hard.

My mother continued to clean house all day, and I spent a great deal of my time outside making mud pies or inside coloring in my coloring books or playing dolls. I was passing time, waiting for my sister to come home from school.

In that house, my sister and I came down with chickenpox. I remember just lying-in bed staring. I remember the bed as a crib. I was too sick to draw or color or play with dolls. My sister became well before me and was able to go back to school. During this time, my mother would be angry with my sister in the mornings; she hit my sister on once or twice that I remember. My sister would cry, then my mom would say she was sorry and give her a hug before she went off to school. I don't remember my mother ever being mean to me. It was very confusing. I felt upset and alone.

Our next move was to the Oregon coast near Siletz Bay. We lived on a dairy farm. My father worked in the logging mill and took care of the cows on the farm. He would get up early in the morning to feed and milk the cows, then go off to work at the mill. When he arrived home from work, he would feed and milk the cows again. We moved to this house during the summer, and my sister and I had so much fun that summer. We had a dog we named "Pie-Y." He was a spotted black, brown, and white herd dog and would help to bring the cows into the barn in the evening. He would follow my sister and me around, never leaving our side. We played in the fields with the cows or in the yard with our dolls. Mom, of course, was in the house cleaning.

It was a hot summer day, my sister and I decided to go exploring out to the end of the pasture. We had never been to the end before, and it seemed like it went on forever. We decided we wanted to see how far it was to the fence we knew must be at the back end of the property line. A fence was necessary to keep the cows in the pasture. We were having fun talking and laughing as we walked along. Pie-Y was following us as usual. We climbed a small hill and stood there in total awe. We were so excited; we couldn't believe what we were looking at. How could it be? We found the ocean! We had no idea we were so close to the ocean, and we were sure our parents didn't know either. We played in the sand for quite a while before we decided we had been gone a long time and our mom would be worrying, so we started heading back home. We talked about telling our parents our exciting news and decided to wait until Dad came home so we could tell them together about our great discovery. We later learned that it was not a surprise to them, and we were instructed to stay away from the beach. We were so 0.19 to watch the baby hummingbirds. They were so tiny. We wanted to pick them up, but Dad said not to because the mother bird may not come back.

Life was good, and I had no worries. Then Mom and Dad started going to church in town close to the dairy farm. My sister and I didn't like the church or the people in the church. We thought they were very strange. They would kneel down at the front altar to pray. Their prayers started out quietly, but soon one or two then more of them would begin moaning and saying things that I couldn't understand. Mom said they were speaking in tongues to God, in the spirit of God. It made no sense to my sister or me. We didn't know what to make of it, and we sure didn't like it. We felt frightened by their actions and the way they spoke. I was always glad when church was over.

My mom began talking to God at home and that frightened me even more. She began to say that the Lord was speaking to her and through her, and he was guiding her. I didn't understand what was going on. All I knew was that I liked my old mother better than this new one. I didn't know what she was talking about when she would speak in Spanish, but that was fun, and I liked it. She hadn't spoken to God like this before, not until after she had joined the church. I decided, even if it was God, I didn't like it. Something changed in our house. There was a feeling of unease in the air. It seemed like there was less happiness and more tension between Mom and Dad.

I woke up on a warm sunny summer morning and found my mother and father carrying all our things out into the yard and dropping them in a pile. Mom said the Lord had told her we were supposed to burn all our "worldly possessions" and drive to Albuquerque, New Mexico. My grandmother (my mom's mother) and my mother's brothers and sisters all lived in Albuquerque, and she said we were going to visit them. I couldn't understand why we had to burn everything before we left on this trip.

We must have been driving for hours. I woke up and was hungry. Dad stopped at a store and bought bread and lunch meat for sandwiches and pop to drink. We ate in the car while Dad kept driving. My mother began singing a song called "Bye Bye Blackbird." I remember her singing that song over and over again. I began to hate that song, and I wished she would stop singing. Dad soon stopped at a gas station so Mom could use the bathroom. Dad was sitting behind the steering wheel, and my sister was sitting next to me in the back seat, just behind Dad. I said, "Dad." He said, "Yea." I said, "Mom's crazy." Dad then answered two words that gave me great comfort. Thank God I wasn't alone anymore. Thank God there was someone to take care of me, my dad. I began to feel happy again. The fear was slipping away. My dad had answered, "I know." A warm feeling came over me. *I'm not alone anymore,* I thought, *my dad knows what I know. Now he can once again take care of me.* But at the same time, deep down inside, I knew I could never again feel as safe as I used to feel. I could never trust my dad or my mom completely the way I used to. I now must always be on guard, looking out for myself.

After days and nights of driving, we were in New Mexico. It was hot, and we were all tired, and Dad pulled off the side of the highway. He announced, "We are out of gas, we are out of food, and we are out of money." Dad said we'd have to get out and walk because it was too hot to just sit there in the car. We headed out across the countryside that looked like a desert to me. There weren't trees and tall grass like there was in Oregon, but the ground was easy to walk on. We walked for hours before it began to get dark. I was so tired, and the darkness was frightening. Dad began to play a game with my sister and me. He pointed up at the stars and told us stories. He pointed to a group of stars and said it was the Big Dipper. We couldn't see it at first. My sister found it first and helped point it out to me. Then once I finally saw it, Dad told us to try to find another one just like it, only smaller. As more stars came out, the sky seemed brighter. I wasn't so afraid anymore, but my sister and I were too tired to keep walking. We told Dad we had to go to the bathroom. He said we had to just go behind a pile of rocks. I found this to be very upsetting. I didn't like not having any toilet paper or water to wash my hands. I didn't like feeing dirty. After a while, I was too tired to care. Dad soon found a sandy clearing and said we'd have to sleep out in the desert that night. Dad cleared the area of rocks, trying to make a smooth spot for us to lie down on. The four of us lay down together. My sister and I were in the middle with my mother and father on the outside. I was next to Dad and my sister was next to Mom. I put my head on my dad's shoulder and my sister snuggled up to me. Dad pointed out more stars and kept talking to us, and soon I was able to fall asleep.

The next morning when I woke, mom and dad were sitting up talking. Mom seemed mad about something. She was mad all the time now and hadn't been talking the last couple of days. Suddenly she took off her wedding rings and threw them off into the desert. I wanted to run to where I thought they landed and try to find them. Mom said to leave them alone. She said she should have thrown them on the fire with the rest of our belongings back home. I remember wishing I could sneak off to find them secretly and keep them for myself. I thought I could maybe sell them for food or clothes. I figured if Mom didn't want them anymore, what difference did it make? Dad said we needed to get started walking before it got too hot. So, there we were, the four of us, me, dad, mom, and sis, walking across the desert. Our clothes were dirty, our hair was dirty and a mess, and we were all hungry and thirsty. This must have been quite a sight to see.

Sometime in the early afternoon, we walked over a hill and could see a town below. Dad said it was Albuquerque. I was so happy because our journey was almost over. Dad said we'd walk to the nearest house and ask if we could use their telephone to call our grandmother. He said Grandma would get one of my mother's brothers to come and pick us up. We walked up to the first house we came to. It was a large white house with a big yard with large trees. Dad knocked while my sister and I waited in the yard with our mom. The door opened and a woman came out. Dad said something to her and then they both went into the house. We waited what seemed a long time because it was so hot there in the sun. Soon Dad came out and walked down off the porch over to where we were waiting. He said, "I talked to William, and he's coming to get us." William is my mother's brother. The lady of the house said for us to go around to the backyard, and she would give us something to eat and drink. We walked around the house and headed for a picnic table sitting under a large tree. We sat down quietly and waited. The lady came out and asked if we would like to go in and wash up. My sister and I got up from the picnic table to go into the house. I don't remember what Mom and Dad did. We went into the bathroom together and washed up. It was nice to be able to go potty in a bathroom. We took turns.

Then my sister helped me wash up. When we were walking through the kitchen toward the back door, I heard the lady say, "Those poor little girls." I felt angry and ashamed. I said to myself, "I'm going to make sure no one says that about me ever again." My sister and I sat down at the table with Mom and Dad, and we began to eat. I don't remember what kind of sandwiches she served; I just remember they were good. As hungry as I was, I would have eaten anything. We stayed out in the back yard waiting for my Uncle William. He finally arrived and took us to Grandma's house.

The first afternoon we were there, my grandmother heated water on the woodstove and filled a round metal tub in the bathroom for my sister and me to take a bath. She had indoor plumbing, but she only had a shower, and we wanted to take a bath. She had clean clothes for us that she must have gotten from one of her other grandchildren. It felt so good to be clean again and to have on clean clothes. My mom once told me that when she was growing up, they had to use an outhouse. We were happy that grandma now had a bathroom inside the house, just off the kitchen.

A few days had passed since we arrived. On this particular day, it was noisy at Grandma's house. Everyone was talking at once. It must have been a Saturday or Sunday because it was early afternoon, and my two uncles, William and Gilbert, were there and not at work, as well as a couple of my mom's sisters, Sally and Sanford. Her sisters Irene and Flora did not live in the same town, so they were not present. They talked in Spanish most of the time since that's the only language my grandmother understood and spoke. Every so often, someone would speak in English to tell my father what the others were saying. My father was trying to convince them that my mother was crazy and needed medical help. I was frightened and confused again. My mother had been acting pretty normal the few days we had been there, but by then, I kept my distance from her, giving all my attention to my grandmother. I remember grandma giving us big hugs. Mom had stopped hugging. Maybe that was because she was mad all the time. My sister and I were sitting in the small living room while the others were seated around a long dining room table talking and what sounded like arguing. Now and then, someone would get up and walk around. My father appeared very frustrated because they wouldn't believe him. After a while, my mother began talking rapidly, not making sense. Everyone became quiet and stared at my mother while she babbled on and on. Sometime later, a van pulled up in front of the house and two men came into the house wearing white coats. They put a white coat with exceptionally long sleeves on my mother. They put the coat on backwards, folded her arms across her chest and tied the sleeves in the back. They had to help her out the front door because she was protesting. She didn't want to go and was begging to stay. I was crying. I didn't want her to go either, but I did want her to get well. I knew she had to go so the doctors could give her the right medicine to get her better. I was scared and angry all at the same time. My dad hugged my sister and me as did my grandmother after Mom and the men in the white coats left. It was scary and sad for me. I didn't know if I would ever see my mom again, but somehow, I knew my mother would never be the same. I felt lost and alone again.

The next week my father left. He said he was moving not too far away to be close to a job he had taken. He promised he would be back on the weekend to see us. Again, that lost and alone feeling came back. A feeling that kept creeping in. I knew our grandmother would take care of us, so that gave me comfort.

My grandmother's name was Candelaria Armijo Gutierrez. My grandfather had passed away years ago, and I never met him. His name was Gabriel Gutierrez. My grandmother lived alone in the same house that my mother and her siblings grew up in. My sister and I spent our days exploring our new home and getting acquainted with our grandmother.

Grandmother's house was made of adobe and was a light tan color. That was the first time I had ever seen an adobe house and I liked it. The walls were very thick, and even when it was hot outside, it remained cool inside. Grandma had Spanish-looking furniture with colorful blankets draped over them. She had a long table in the dining room that was just past the living room and to the left of the kitchen. Instead of chairs on the sides of the table, there were two long benches. The chairs on the ends of the table seemed exceptionally large, much too big for my sister and me to sit in. I liked sitting on my knees on the bench when I colored in my coloring book. There were three bedrooms.

The bedroom my sister and I slept in was large and had several beds in it. I figured my mother, and her sisters must have slept in this room since there were four of them. Her two brothers must have slept in the other bedroom nearby and her parents in the bedroom off by itself. I used to try to imagine what it was like to have such a large family—to have all those beds and such a long table. It must have been fun growing up there.

I especially liked Grandma's kitchen. It was always warm; it always smelled of food cooking, and there were strings of chili and garlic hanging from hooks to dry. Grandma made fresh tortillas every day. I loved those the most. I liked eating my food with pieces of tortilla instead of with a fork or spoon. It was messy but fun. I always had to have a glass of water nearby when I ate Grandma's food. It was hot with chili. I couldn't understand how she could eat such hot food and not have to drink water. Even with water, my mouth would burn.

My grandmother was sweet and loving. She also was funny, I thought. Grandma couldn't speak English very well. She seemed to understand a little English when she heard it, but she had trouble speaking it. Or I only thought she understood me. Perhaps when she shook her head up and down, she really didn't know what I was talking about. We spent time laughing at each other, trying to understand what the other person was saying.

One day my sister and I were sitting out on the large wood swing by the flower garden. We spent a great deal of time on that swing. I had never seen one like it before. It was more like a wood couch with a long seat, back and sides made out of wood, supported by a wood frame. When my sister and I sat on it together, there was room for someone else. Anyway, we were swinging back and forth when our grandmother came out of the house and called to us. We went running to see what she wanted. She pointed to the sprinkler on the front lawn, and she said, "Turn around the water." My sister and I looked at each other, then looked at Grandma, and she repeated, with a puzzled look on her face, "Turn around the water?" Grandma was smiling and nodding her head. My sister and I looked at each other again and slowly walked over to the sprinkler. We then took a deep breath and proceeded to twirl and dance around and around in the water that was spraying out from the sprinkler. Grandma began to shout, "No! No, turn around the water!" This time she was making a twisting motion with her hand and wrist as if twisting off a lid. My sister and I began to laugh, and then Grandma began to laugh. My sister and I shouted, "Oh, turn the water off!" Grandma again nodded her head up and down while she said, "Si!" We ran and turned off the water for Grandma so she could move the sprinkler to a dry spot, then we turned the water back on for her. When we ran back to her, she gave us both a big hug and ushered us into the house so we could change our clothes.

Grandma wore her hair in a bun on the back of her head. I had never seen it down, and one evening I asked her if I could brush her hair. I always liked brushing hair. Not my hair, other people's hair. My dad would let me do it all the time, but not my mother, though I would ask her from time to time. She said she didn't want her hair messed up even though I tried to convince her that I was going to make it pretty. I was so excited that my grandma was going to let me brush her hair. I had never brushed long hair before. She sat on a stool in front of her dressing table and took out the pins that held her bun in place. I couldn't believe my eyes when I saw that her hair fell all the way down her back and rested on the edge of the stool on which she was sitting. It was too long for me to try any new styles, but I enjoyed brushing it over, and over again. I could tell she enjoyed it too.

Our hot summer days at grandmother's house were spent playing outside, and when it got too hot to play even in the shade, we'd go inside and color or play with dolls or help Grandma with chores. Grandma didn't drive, so the only time we went anywhere during the week was when one of our aunts would visit to take Grandma shopping. They would sometimes take us to their house.

Before long, it was September, and school started. Mom was still in the hospital, and Dad was still working in another town. We only saw him on weekends. So, Grandma enrolled us in school. I started kindergarten and my sister was in the second grade. We were so happy to find that the teacher spoke English and all the students spoke English. That is, until we went outside to play. Once outside on the playground, everyone spoke Spanish. I felt that lonely feeling again. I had no one to play with. No one would talk to me during recess. I felt so alone, and I soon learned my sister felt the same way. I only saw her during noon recess, and we would just walk around together. One day, after a couple of weeks of school, my sister and I were talking about how we hated school and living in this place where we couldn't understand the language, and no one would teach it to us. We both decided we wanted to move back to Oregon. We wanted to see our grandparents in Oregon. We missed Grammer and Poppy as we called them. They were our dad's parents. We decided we would try to talk dad into moving back to Oregon the next weekend he visited us. We knew if we begged him, he would take us back to Oregon. As it turned out, he lost his job and had been thinking about moving back to Oregon anyway as he believed there were more job opportunities for him there. He could always find work in a sawmill or for a logging company in Oregon.

We left for Oregon the following Sunday. We packed the few clothes we had accumulated, gave Grandma a big hug and kiss and headed for Oregon. Little did we know we would never see Grandma Gutierrez again, but I knew I would never forget her or the time I spent with her in her cool adobe house.

We were riding in the car with the windows rolled down. It was so hot, and we were trying to keep cool, so we leaned our heads towards the window. My sister was in the front seat, and I was in the back seat doing the same thing. We could ride along like this for hours. We never worried about our hair getting tangled; we only wanted to get cool. It was so uncomfortably hot.

We stopped in a town in Northern California, and Dad stopped to get a motel room for the night. It was a single room with two beds, two chairs and a black and white television. There was a nightstand by each bed with a single lamp on each one. The windows had metal venetian blinds and curtains you could pull shut to make the room dark during the day. After we checked into the motel, Dad took us to a nearby restaurant for dinner. Then he took us back to the motel. He said he was going out for a while and for us to keep the door locked. My sister and I watched television until we were too sleepy to keep our eyes open. She and I slept in one bed together. Sometime in the middle of the night, we heard Dad stumble in. He fell into bed and begin to snore. We could smell alcohol. I was frightened, so my sister hugged me. I soon fell back asleep.

The next morning my sister and I watched television again. Only this time, we had the volume turned down low so we wouldn't wake up Dad. He finally woke up and took us to the restaurant again for breakfast. We thought we were going to continue to Oregon, but when we got back to the room, Dad gave my sister money and said he'd be back in a little while. He said if we got hungry before he returned, we could just walk to the restaurant again and eat. My sister and I watched television all day long. We had nothing else to do. We pulled the curtains shut so the sun wouldn't shine in the room and just sat or lay on our bed and stared at the television, changing channels every so often. It was late in the afternoon, and we were both getting very hungry. My sister said we should walk to the restaurant. I was afraid to go. I was afraid to walk along the street, and I was afraid we would get lost. I remember thinking I wish I had paid more attention when we walked to the restaurant that morning. I wasn't sure how to get there. My sister reassured me that she knew where it was and that we wouldn't get lost. So, the two of us walked out the door of the motel, locked it with the extra key Dad had left for us and headed for the restaurant. My sister was almost seven years old; I was just five. We walked hand in hand down the street in the strange town in Northern California. I kept hoping we wouldn't get lost because I didn't know the name of the motel, and I was too afraid to ask my sister if she remembered. We made it to the restaurant, walked in and headed for a booth toward the back of the narrow restaurant and slid in quietly. There were booths along the wall of windows on one side and a counter on the other side where people could sit. I was so frightened to be there. I was afraid someone would try to snatch us. I knew it was wrong for us to be in this strange place all by ourselves.

My sister ordered for us. I couldn't read the menu, so she listed off items that she knew I would like. We quickly ate, and my sister put money on the table when the waitress brought us our bill. I was glad when the waitress came back to give us our change at the table, as we had planned to get up and move quickly out the door before anyone had a chance to stop us. We didn't want to have to stop at the cash register on the way out. We both half-walked, half-ran back to the motel, and I was so glad to see the front door to our room. We quickly entered the room, shut, and locked the door behind us, and I took a deep breath. I began to feel safe again, but not for long. We proceeded to watch television again and wait for Dad to return. We had no idea where he was and why he left us locked up in the motel room all day. We desperately wanted to leave for Oregon. When we got so sleepy, we couldn't keep our eyes open, we turned off the television and went to bed. It was late when we heard Dad stumble in again. The smell of alcohol was very strong. We heard him take off his clothes and stumble into bed. I felt very frightened but soon felt better when I heard him snoring. Sometime in the middle of the night, Dad got up and stumbled over to our bed and sat down on my side of the bed. I could just barely see him in the dim light and what I saw frightened me. He muttered something that didn't make sense and began pulling the covers off me. At that moment, my sister pulled me toward her, and we both ran for the bathroom. Once inside, we locked the door and stood there in the dark, holding one another. We waited and listened. It seemed like the longest time, but finally, we heard Dad snoring. We were afraid to leave the bathroom, so we decided to sleep on the floor. We spread a towel down on the floor and lay down together, spreading another towel over us. It was cold at first, but we snuggled together and were soon asleep. We woke up with a start the next morning to Dad pounding on the bathroom door. We were frightened. We thought we were going to be in trouble. We quickly hung up the towels and opened the door. Our dad rushed in as we rushed out. He shut the door to use the bathroom. When he came out of the bathroom, we were sitting together on the bed. He asked us if we were all right. We both said, "Yes." He asked us why we slept in the bathroom, and we said we were afraid. Dad then said, "It's time to get in the car and head for Oregon." My sister and I were happy to be leaving that motel room. I was no longer feeling fear. Dad said we should be arriving at our grandparents before evening, and that's what I was happy about. I didn't want to spend another night alone with Dad. I was afraid he'd go out drinking again, and even though he said he was sorry and wouldn't drink anymore, I didn't believe him. I just kept thinking he shouldn't have left us alone in that motel room. As young as I was, I knew it was wrong.

Late that afternoon, we were pulling up at our grandparents' farm in Stayton, Oregon. We got out of the car and went running to our grandmother, who was standing on the front porch to greet us. We called to Grammer, and she had hugs and kisses for us. Our grandfather, Poppy, was out on the farm. He came walking into the house soon after. I knew life would be good and safe again, at least for a while, as long as we stayed with Grammer and Poppy.

Soon we were all sitting around the dining room table, and Grammer was feeding us. She looked at my hair and my sister's hair and said, "Oh my God, the first thing we will need to do is cut your hair since I know we won't ever be able to remove all those tangles." I felt safe again.

Mom & Dad Dating

Mom Holding Gloria &
Dad Holding Florence

Mom & Her two Precious girls

Florence holding Gloria

The Barn on the property where
our belongings were burned

# II
## "College – A Dream"

I was eight years old the first time I thought about college. My sister and I were living in San Diego with our Aunt Marion and Uncle Jack. It was another one of those times (and they happened nearly every year) when our mother was in the mental hospital, but this time Dad was in jail. He had to serve a year jail sentence for a hit and run accident he was involved in one night when he was driving drunk. We were living in Eureka, California, at the time. I remember the accident well. It was a Friday night and payday for Dad. There was often nothing to eat in the house the last day before payday. We were waiting for Dad to come home so we could go grocery shopping. We would watch the clock with anxiety, all the time wondering would he come straight home or stop off at the tavern first? If he stopped off at a tavern, we knew it would be late before he would arrive home, and we would have to wait with hunger in our stomachs and fear on our faces. We worried that he might be mad and fight with Mom. Mom would always get very short-tempered on these occasions. My sister and I made a point to stay out of her way when Dad was late.

This particular Friday night, he came home around seven o'clock and, yes, he had been drinking. He said he was going to the grocery store and told me to come with him. I don't know why I was the chosen one. I was terribly upset and nervous. I didn't want to go to the store with him. I never liked to be around Dad when he had been drinking. His voice was always loud, and he'd be happy one minute and angry the next. I hated him when he drank. I did want to eat dinner, though.

We shopped for groceries at a small local store. Afterward, I got into the car on the passenger side while Dad got into the driver's side and placed the bag of groceries in the front seat between us. We pulled out from the curb and began driving down the road, when all of a sudden, we scraped the side of another car. Dad went over the centerline and sideswiped an oncoming car. I was too small to see out the window very well, but he hit the car on his side of our car. He cussed and kept driving. We went a couple of blocks, then turned the corner, and he pulled over. We sat in the car for a few minutes then he asked me if I was all right. I was too scared to speak, so I just nodded. Then Dad said we'd better go back and make sure no one in the other car was hurt. We made a full circle around the block until we were once again in front of the grocery store but on the opposite side of the road. Dad pulled over and stopped. There were two police officers there. One of them walked over to the car and asked Dad to get out. One of the police officers came over to my side of the car and told me that they had to take my dad. I got out of the car and picked up the bag of groceries. I remember my dad saying that I could just walk home, that it wasn't too far. I was seven years old with what seemed like a large bag of groceries. I started walking home, and after a step or two, the tears began to stream down my face. A young girl and a young man walked over to me and asked if I wanted them to walk me home. I just shook my head no and kept on walking. After a while, I realized they were walking a short distance behind me. As I walked down the dark sidewalk with my large bag of groceries, I was glad they were there. They made me feel safe, these two strangers walking behind me. We were living in a housing project at the time and when I turned the corner to enter the project, the couple kept walking straight. I was frightened again because it was so very dark, and I had never been out walking at night by myself before. I knew that I shouldn't be out there alone. I hoped no one would see me or try to grab me. The shadows and noises of the night frightened me. I finally reached our door and knocked. When Mom opened the door, I started crying uncontrollably. She asked where Dad was and why was I crying. She lifted the groceries from my weary little arms, set the bag down and asked, "What happened? Where's your dad?" I could tell she was getting upset with me, but I couldn't talk; I just kept crying. Finally, she shook me hard back and forth and said to stop crying and to tell her what happened. I was then able to blurt out the story of the traffic incident and that the police had taken Dad away in the police car.

We would go to the jail every Saturday after that to visit Dad. Since Mom never learned to drive, we would take a cab to the City Jail and talk to Dad through a telephone with a glass window between us. I hated those visits. I hated seeing Dad like that, and I never had anything to say. He did seem in good spirits, and he would always joke with us. I missed him and wished he were home with us.

My sister and I finished out the school year. Dad was still in jail, and we were weeks into summer when my sister and I noticed that our mother was becoming ill again. We stopped visiting our dad. Mom seemed to be angry all the time. My sister and I would be gone from the apartment for hours just being outside or exploring. We didn't want to be hanging around when Mom got mad. It was one of those government housing projects where all the buildings look alike from the outside. Our apartment came sparsely furnished. I remember the living room, kitchen, and dining room were all in one room with linoleum floors. There were two bedrooms. My sister and I always shared a room. The floor in the bedrooms was covered with linoleum, and in the winter, the floors were very cold. We had rollup shades on the windows and plastic curtains. As sparse and ugly as it was, it was typical of the places I remember living in growing up with my parents.

The three of us were having an early dinner one summer afternoon. My mom was talking in an angry voice when I asked her why she was angry. She immediately picked up a plate of food and threw it at me. It missed me and hit the floor behind me. I didn't say a word through the rest of dinner, and neither did my sister. Afterward, we went into our bedroom and shut the door. My sister and I began discussing Mom. My sister said, "Mom's getting sick again." I asked her, "What should we do?" We just sat there on our twin beds staring at each other. Pretty soon, my sister said, "Let's call Grammer and Poppy." I liked that idea. I knew Grammer and Poppy would think of something. Since we didn't have a telephone, we decided to walk to the grocery store, which had a phone booth on the corner outside. We took all the money we had in our piggy banks because we didn't know how much the phone call would cost. We were in northern California, and our grandparents were in Oregon. We told our mom we were going to the store to buy candy and that we'd be right back. When we arrived at the store, we dumped out all our change and asked the store clerk to give us quarters because we needed to use the telephone outside. It took the clerk time to count out all our dimes, nickels and pennies and convert the change to quarters. With our pocket full of quarters, we went into the phone booth. I was glad my sister was taller than me because I couldn't reach the telephone to put the money in. My sister talked to our grandmother first, then she let me talk to her for a minute before taking the phone back. Grandma asked if I was all right. She said everything was going to be okay and for me to do what my sister told me to do. Then she said to hand the phone to my sister. I was so anxious to find out what Grandma had said to my sister. When my sister told me that Grandma said to call the police and tell them where we were, why we were calling and ask them to come and get us, I was very frightened again. She said to tell them our dad was in the City Jail; our mother was sick, and our grandparents were coming to get us, but they wouldn't arrive until the next day. I was so scared. I was so afraid Mom would be worried if we didn't go right back home, but at the same time, I knew we couldn't go back home. I was afraid to go home and afraid not to go home. My sister called the police. We were told to stay by the phone booth, and they would send an officer to come and get us. When the police arrived, I felt so embarrassed getting into the back seat of the patrol car with my sister. I remember thinking only criminals ride in the back seat of police cars. The police officer was so nice that I was soon was less afraid.

We arrived at the City Jail, and the police officer walked us inside and showed us where to sit and wait. Soon another officer came and told us to follow him into another office. The officer sitting in the office behind a big desk asked us to sit down. We chose to both sit in the same chair since it was so big. The officer sitting behind the big desk told us he had talked to our father and our grandparents. He said they had sent someone to our apartment to pick up our mom. He said she was okay, and that they were transporting her to the American Lake Hospital in Washington, where she would get help so she could get better.

Since Mom had been in the Army when she was young, she qualified for the Veterans Hospital, free of charge. Every time she got sick, which was whenever she stopped taking her pills, she would be sent off to the American Lake Hospital in Washington. This happened almost yearly as previously stated. I was four and a half until I was fourteen. I was seven when this happened, and this was the third time she was going there to get better.

I told the officer that was where my mom would want to go

because she always got better when she went to that hospital. I told him I thought she just needed a rest. The officer said that since our grandparents couldn't arrive to get us until the next morning, we would have to spend the night in the girls' detention center because they had no place for us to stay. They said they would have a special room for us so we would be separate from all the other girls at the center. I really didn't like that idea, and I felt frightened again. I was glad my sister was holding my hand during all this time. Shortly after, a woman police officer came into the room and told us to follow her. She put us in the back seat of a patrol car. She said she was driving us to the girls' detention center, that it wasn't far, and we would be safe there.

When we arrived at the detention center, we were escorted into a room with two twin beds and an adjoining bathroom. There was wire mesh in the glass windows and bars over that. I felt relieved and less tense at this point. They gave us comic books to look at and said they would bring us something to eat. They shut the door, and I heard the lock turn. We were locked in our rooms and that made me feel safe. My sister and I looked through the comic books until we heard the lock turn, and the door open. Someone brought us two trays of food along with nightclothes, toothbrushes, and toothpaste. I remember them telling us that they were sorry they had to lock the door, but they wanted to make sure we were safe. Someone would be on duty just down the hall all night long. We shouldn't be afraid. I don't remember what we ate, but when we finished, they came back and took the trays. They told us we had to get ready for bed; they were going to have to turn the lights out soon.

It had been a long day, and I soon fell asleep, only to be awakened with a start in the early morning as I heard girls talking in loud voices. The voices were coming from across the courtyard outside our window. It frightened me, and I realized that I had wet the bed during the night. I got up and got in bed with my sister. She hugged me and told me not to worry and not to be afraid. Her bed was on the other side of the room from the window. I was afraid those girls would try to beat us up. Their voices sounded so harsh and mean. We stayed in bed and talked. An attendant soon came in and told us to get washed up and dressed because they were bringing us breakfast soon. After breakfast, we just sat on the bed and looked at comic books patiently waiting for our grandparents to come for us. The time went by ever so slowly; I thought they would never arrive. I was so excited when the door opened and in walked our grandparents. After hugs and kisses, we were in their car heading for their farm in Oregon. I was so happy, and once again, I felt safe.

We stayed with our grandparents until Aunt Marion and Uncle Jack arrived from San Diego. It was two weeks before Marion and Jack drove up. Jack had to take time off from work. Marion and Jack said they wanted to take us San Diego to San Diego to live with them and asked if that was okay with us. We were so excited to live with them. They had always been so nice to us, and we loved them dearly.

Marion and Jack had a son, Larry. He was one year younger than me, but we were both born on Valentine's Day, so we thought we had a special bond between us. We soon settled into Marion and Jack's home. The house was small and had only two bedrooms, so Marion and Jack gave us their bedroom. They slept on the couch in the living room. They didn't seem to mind at all. After a while, we felt like one happy family. My sister and I didn't miss our parents or our grandparents. We were living a normal life for the first time. We lived in a nice house in a nice neighborhood. We wore nice clothes and always had plenty to eat. We were both safe and happy. I was able to do all the things the other kids in school got to do because there wasn't any shortage of money. I went to Camp Palomar for a week with my class. I had so much fun swimming in the lake, taking hikes, playing games, visiting the Palomar Conservatory, and just having fun with my friends.

Coming back from that field trip on the school bus, we went past a community college in San Diego. I stared out the window, looking at the older students walking with books in their arms or backpacks on their back, heading to various classrooms. At that moment, I said to myself, *I am going to college someday. That is what I really want to do.* I loved school. I always did. School was a place I could excel. When at school, I could hide from my home life. I didn't feel different from the other kids when I was at school. This was a promise I made to myself. Somehow, I would go to college. I don't know where, but I only knew that I would attend a college sometime in my life. I was going to make sure I could take care of myself. I soon forgot this pledge.

Grammer & Poppy

Aunt Marion & Uncle Jack

High School Graduation

High School Graduation
Walking with Daren

# III
## "Helping Hands"

The year went by way too fast. Soon, school was out for the summer. Dad was also out of jail, and he wanted us to come back to Oregon. My sister and I didn't want to go back to live with Dad, but we were afraid to say anything. Our grandparents arrived and loaded us up in the car, and we headed to Oregon to stay with our grandparents through the summer while our dad found work and a place for us to live. It was a sad trip for my sister and me. We adapted. Even though we missed our aunt and uncle and our life in San Diego, my sister and I enjoyed staying with our grandparents. They were always fun to be around.

Poppy worked in the local cannery in Stayton and worked his farm in the evenings and on weekends. He always wore bib overalls and would often hide peppermints in one of his breast pockets. Sometimes when I climbed up in his lap in the evening, he would reach into his pocket and hand me one. Poppy also had false teeth that he didn't like to wear. He would say they hurt his mouth. He would wear them when he ate, but when I'd go to kiss him good night when his teeth were out. His kisses were very juicy when he wasn't wearing his teeth in. I used to tease him about how I liked his kisses better without his teeth. He was such a loving man. He had a shop out back and would go out there to make things out of wood. One Christmas, I remember he made a small box for my sister and me. It was round and stained and varnished with our names on the front. The box also had a lid. I loved that box and used it for my treasures. Another time when we were visiting, I asked him to make another one for me. This time it was square with a lid with a hinge. It was stained and varnished. I still have the box to this day and treasure it because it reminds me of how loving he was.

Grammer stayed home. She never worked outside of the home because she had seven children, and that was enough work to keep her busy. I remember hearing that Grammer suffered from migraine headaches, and during those episodes, her disposition was very unpleasant. She stayed in bed during this time. They lived in Iowa until a tornado flattened their home. The story told to me was they packed the old Ford with all their belongings inside and on the top of the car. There was barely room for all of them to sit. They all arrived in Stayton, Oregon, with just a handful of dollars in their pockets. They managed to find a place to live. Poppy got a job in the cannery right away. Eventually, they bought the farm in West Stayton, and that's the place they lived when I was little. The farm had a barn, cows, sheep, a dog, a large garden, fruit trees, a chicken coop with chickens and two cats. There was always adventure on the farm and always work to do. Poppy also grew a type of grass used for hay, and it was so much fun playing in the bales of hay in the barn loft.

Grammer was a great cook. I used to love the way she would set the table for a meal. When my sister and I were at home with our parents, a meal consisted of one or two items, but when Grammer planned a meal, well, it was sometimes hard to count all the different types of food. Always some kind of meat, a salad, potatoes, biscuits or rolls, jelly, pickles, tomatoes, and olives were on the table. I was told this is how the farmers ate back in the Midwest. They worked hard in the fields, and the work was so tiring, they needed the extra food. In the summer, Grammer canned pickles, fruit, meat, and many types of vegetables, and she always had a pantry full of jars of food. Sometimes I would go into the pantry to just look at all the canned food.

Grammer loved to watch wrestling on Friday nights. She would make a big batch of popcorn, and we'd settle down to watch the fights. Grammer would get all fired up when the match was on. She had her favorites and would yell at the TV screen if her favorite wrestlers weren't winning.

We stayed with Poppy and Grammer off and on from when I was five until I was eleven or twelve. Mom would stop taking her pills and have to go back to American Lake Hospital. My sister and I would end up staying with Poppy and Grammer off and on for a couple of months or weeks at a time. This went on year after year. We didn't always stay with Grammer and Poppy. Sometimes when Mom was in the hospital, Dad would have a girlfriend, and he would move her in with us. My sister and I hated his girlfriends, but we agreed life was better when they were around. Dad would stay home more and not go out drinking. The girlfriend would help clean the house and cook. I guess you could say we tolerated his girlfriends because we knew that as soon as Mom came home, they would be gone.

The last time Mom went into the hospital, I was in the eighth grade, and my sister was a sophomore in high school. We lived in a shack next to a Grange Hall in a small town in Oregon called Lyons. That's when I became friends with Sharlene and Marge. Marge lived just down the street from me, and Sharlene lived just a little farther away down by the river. We met while we were in the seventh grade and formed a friendship that lasted a lifetime. On Saturdays I would walk to Marge's house, and the two of us would walk together to Sharlene's house. Sharlene had a deep-fry machine, and we would make french fries. We would sit down and talk while eating french fries and drinking Coca-Cola. We spent many a Saturday afternoon doing this.

One Saturday afternoon Dad found a fawn caught in the fence behind hour house and brought it inside. The fawn's mother took off in a fast run, but the fawn couldn't follow because he was caught in the fence. We took care of the fawn for three weeks or more. One summer day, Dad said we had to untie the fawn because the game warden was coming to our house to check on a rumor. He heard we had a fawn tied up in our yard. I learned it was against the law to pen up a wild animal. When the game warden showed up, the fawn was gone. I was so glad we didn't get into trouble. I was afraid they would take Dad to jail.

One evening the next winter evening I remember hearing a sound on the front porch. It sounded a little like pounding or tapping. I opened the door, and there was a large deer with antlers staring me in the face. I opened the door wide and stepped back as the adult deer stepped into the living room. All of us hugged, kissed, and petted the deer before we opened the door and watched him walk away. I was so thrilled to know the fawn survived and remembered us. I'd like to believe we saved his life. At any rate, it was quite an evening for us and one happy memory I will never forget.

Graduation from the eighth grade was just around the corner

when I developed a terrible stomachache during the evening. My dad had taken me and Sharlene out to a movie, and on the way home, I was in a great deal of pain. We took Sharlene home, and I went to bed as soon as we arrived home. I didn't sleep well. The next morning, I woke up, got out of bed, and walked just four steps before I fainted. I remember Dad helping me up and putting me back to bed. He pushed on my stomach, and it was very painful. He said it was probably my appendix. Dad left soon after, saying he wouldn't be gone long, and he would come back to check on me. That was about 9:30 in the morning. It must have been 4:00 pm or later when he finally came home. I was in so much pain and had been all day. He pushed on my stomach again, and I groaned from the pain. He said he knew it was my appendix, so my sister and I got into the car, and Dad drove us to the hospital. I couldn't stand up straight because the pain was so intense. I wound up having an operation that early evening to have my appendix removed. They determined my appendix had burst when I fainted that morning, resulting in a considerable amount of pus around the stomach area. I spent a couple of days in the hospital and then went to my grandmother's house for a week so she could take care of me. I believe I could have died. Dad had spent the entire day at the bar drinking instead of taking care of me.

I was back home for a week when Dad came home very drunk one night. My sister was out on a date, and I was home alone in bed. Sometime after he went to bed, he got up and came into my bedroom. He was naked and came over to my bed and removed the covers. I began fighting him off and eventually started screaming. He finally let go of me, and I ran out of the bedroom screaming. He came to where I was and said to stop screaming and go back to bed. He said he was sorry and wouldn't bother me anymore. I went back to bed, but I couldn't sleep. When my sister came home from her date, I told her what had happened. She held me while I finally fell asleep. I made my plan. If it ever happened again, I would hurt him with whatever I could find to use as a club. Then I would contact the police and make sure he went to jail. But it never happened again.

I remember Dad coming home drunk another night, and sometime the next day, a police car pulled up outside. Dad crawled out the back window and hid. When the police knocked on the door, we said our father was not home. After the police left, he got into his car and took off. A week went by, and he hadn't returned. There was no food in the house, and my sister and I were getting hungry. We had no idea when he would come home. We knew we couldn't continue to stay home by ourselves. We went next door to use the neighbor's phone because we didn't have one. We called Grammer. Within minutes, our Aunt Helen, who lived not too far from us, came and picked us up. We lived with her during the summer months. We had fun during that summer because we had five cousins to enjoy and hang out with. I didn't feel alone anymore. We also had plenty to eat. I found out that our relatives had packed up everything in the house and put it into storage. They contacted our mother and told her where we were. Our mother always wrote to us when she was in the hospital, and we wrote back, telling her where we were and that we were okay so she wouldn't worry.

As soon as Mom was released, she rented a small apartment in town for the three of to live. The apartment was above the small grocery store. I thought the place was old and ugly with ugly furniture and cold linoleum floors. Regardless, the three of us were happy because Dad wasn't with us, and he wasn't causing trouble like he always did when he drank.

During my sophomore year, my sister got pregnant, and she and Allen married. They moved into a small apartment in Stayton and then it was just my mom and me living in the apartment. Both my sister and Allen remained in high school until they graduated. They were in love and seemed to be so happy. Everyone thought they were so cute and admired them for continuing their education. I missed my sister, but I was happy for her. I remember thinking, *she got out. She is free from this family. Someday I will also be free and won't have to live with anxiety anymore in a family where I don't feel like I belong.*

During my junior year, Dad came back. He was different. He was very overweight and didn't work. He sat around drinking coffee and talking about the bible. Often, he didn't make sense. I didn't like him being there, and I wished he would leave. One day my parents announced we were going to move to Salem. I was devastated because

I didn't want to go to a different high school. I had already gone to ten or eleven different grade schools, and I just wanted to go to one high school. I was so tired of moving. The following day I mentioned to my girlfriend, Kristine, that my parents wanted to move to Salem, and I didn't want to move with them. She said I could come and stay with her and her parents because they had lots of room. I told her to ask her parents, and I would ask mine. The next day she said her mom said it was fine. So, I moved in with Kristine and her parents, and my parents moved to Salem. That was the last time I ever lived with them. I was so happy to be free of them. I had a fun time with Kristine and her family. Kristine was a year older than me, so when I finished my junior year and she graduated from high school, we spent the summer having so much fun. Kristine had her license and a car, so I would ride with her into Salem to our separate jobs during the week, and on the weekend, we would party and visit friends. Her family members were so kind to me and made me feel so welcome when I attended all their family gatherings.

# IV
# Mayme LaVoy

I have Mayme LaVoy to thank for providing me the support I had never experienced. Mayme LaVoy was the girl's counselor and business teacher at Stayton Union High School and had been working at the school for years. During my freshman year, I would hear girls talk about Mrs. Lavoy in a way that made me feel I never wanted to take a class from her or run into her at school. The girls would say that she could be very stern; you didn't ever want to do anything that would cause her to get mad at you.

I made it through my freshman year of high school without ever having a run-in with Mrs. LaVoy; however, during the first quarter of my sophomore year, I signed up for a business class that she was teaching. I was dreading this class but decided to be quiet, study hard, get a good grade, and get out without any interaction with her. After a couple of weeks passed, I was feeling relieved that I had had no contact with Ms. LaVoy. Soon it all changed. She gave us an assignment that changed my life in high school and further on into my future. She asked the class to write an essay on whether we received everything we asked for and how we reacted when we didn't receive what we asked for from our parents. I was determined to do well on this project; therefore, I put a great deal of thought into the assignment before I started writing. I always this in an effort into doing well in school because school was where I felt the same as everyone else. When I was at home, I felt lonely, isolated, and poor. At first, I was confused as to what to write because I realized I never really asked for much, so this would be a difficult assignment. It took me quite a while to start the writing part. Finally, I wrote about how I generally got everything I asked for because I rarely asked for anything. I explained that my parents were extremely poor and couldn't afford extras, so there was no reason to ask for things I knew I wouldn't be able to get. I wrote that prior to asking for anything, I evaluated the cost and the likelihood of my parents being able to provide it for me.

Then I would rarely mention to them what I wanted, as I often felt they couldn't afford to buy it. I ended my essay with the thought that I felt surprisingly good about generally getting what I asked for.

To my joy, I got an "A" on the paper. Mrs. LaVoy asked me to come to her office during my free period. I had no idea what to expect, but I hoped that I would not be in trouble for anything, even though I had no idea what I could possibly be in trouble for. Much to my surprise, Mrs. LaVoy told me that she really liked my essay and asked me if I'd like to work for the school superintendent during my free period at school. She explained I would receive pay plus three class credits. I was so surprised and thrilled to have a part-time job plus receive class credit. The superintendent's office was in a small building across the street from the school. She walked me over to the building and introduced me to the secretary, Irene Morey. From that time on until I graduated from high school, I either worked for the school superintendent or Mrs. Lavoy either one or two class periods during the school day, receiving both payment and class credit. I used some of the money to buy school supplies and clothes and put the rest into a savings account.

The next day the school secretary asked me if I'd like to clean her house on Saturdays to earn extra money. She knew I had no transportation since my mom did not drive and my dad had skipped town the prior year, so she said she would come by and pick me up at 9:00 a.m. each Saturday and take me to her house. This weekend job lasted until I moved to Stayton to live with Kristine the fourth quarter of my junior year. This gave me extra pocket money that I never had before. Now I was able to walk to the local Gingerbread House with my girlfriends on weekends and have money just like they did. This was a major change for me. With money to spend, I felt so much more like everyone else. I always wanted to feel like everyone else, but I always felt different. I was always embarrassed about the places we lived, about my mom not being able to drive, about my dad not providing for us, for taking off and just abandoning us, about so many things in my life.

Mrs. LaVoy took me under her wing the rest of my high school days. From that time on, I always had a job and always had money in my pocket. Away from home, I felt just like everyone else, but when I would go home, reality would set in. I used to wonder how I wound up with the parents I had. I kept thinking there was mistake made. I loved them, but I wanted things to be so different from what they were.

My high school years were fun when I was not worried about something or feeling lonely. I excelled in school; I had close friends, and I partied with my friends, but always studied except for Friday and Saturday nights. I always managed to have friends who had access to a car, and back then, we always went out in groups. We would go to the school's football or basketball game in a car full of girls and often take off early and just drive around or find a party to attend. Everyone drank beer at our gatherings. There were times when my girlfriends also had boyfriends, and I didn't. During those times, I stayed home, which was boring and lonely.

Toward the end of my junior year of school, I told Mrs. LaVoy I didn't want to work in the local cannery during the summer months. In the town of Stayton and the surrounding small towns in Oregon, most kids worked out in the fields picking strawberries and green beans once we were fifteen years old. It was demanding work; however, if we wanted to see our friends, we worked out in the fields since most everyone did. That was the typical kind of work there was for us to do and to sit around all summer was dreadfully boring. I tried babysitting once or twice, but I found that terribly boring. The children would go to bed early, and all I could do was sit and watch television. One time the husband came home drunk and drove me home. That was the last time I babysat. I could stay home if I wanted to be around a drunk. The summer after my sophomore year, I was old enough to work in the cannery. I was assigned to the swing shift along with my other girlfriends. This was great for me because now I had a ride to work. However, I hated working in the cannery. It was bean season and the whole cannery smelled of green beans. Our job was working on the conveyor belt removing rotten beans and foreign objects. It was so tedious just standing in front of the belt watching the beans move along while picking out the rejects. We had to wear hairnets, which I hated, and long gloves. During lunchtime, we'd meet in the lunchroom to eat. That was the only enjoyable time. We'd all sit around eating our lunch talking about what young girls talk about, mostly boys. There were times when I would get so tired just staring at the belt that I would actually fall asleep. I'd wake up, and my arms would be moving back and forth, but I knew I had been asleep. I probably wasn't the only one who succumbed to sleep on the swing shift.

So, as I said before, I told Mrs. LaVoy I didn't want to work in the cannery again because it was too dirty and too boring, and I asked her to help me find another job. Mrs. LaVoy set me up to go to Oregon State during that summer through the Head Start Summer Program. This program was designed to get students interested in college. After one week, I asked Kristine to please drive to Corvallis and pick me up because I hated it there. The students were extremely immature and stupid acting. After I got back, I called Mrs. LaVoy to tell her that I quit and explained why. I told her if you want to turn someone off from going to college, send them there for the summer. I thought she would be mad at me, but she wasn't. She just said, well, you will need a job now. She said she'd call me the next day. She called me on Monday morning to tell me she had a job for me at the State Capital working in the Labor and Industries building in Salem. It was an administrative type of job. The next day Kristine drove me to Salem and dropped me off at the State Capital. I walked to the Labor and Industries building. Kristine worked in Salem as well, so it was very convenient for both of us. I loved working there. Work was fun, and the people were genuinely nice to me. I ran into a girl I remembered from high school. We would have lunch together every day, and we got to know each other well. She was beautiful, and I wondered why her husband hadn't been good to her. As I remember, he drank and stayed out late often and that's why she left him. She was two years older than me, but we hit it off and became friends. She got married right after high school. Now she was divorced and was raising a child by herself. I felt so grownup when I was around her, and she commented on how mature I was. One time she asked me if I'd like to go to Eugene with her to a party. I was so excited. I couldn't believe that she wanted me to go with her. I went home with her after work, and we soon left for Eugene. She took me around the campus so I could see what it looked like, and then we headed for the party. Friends of hers were giving the party in their apartment. It was so much fun. Everyone was so nice. We drank beer, shared stories and laughed. After the party ended and everyone went home, she and I spent the night with her girlfriends. The next day, on the way back to Stayton, she asked me if I wanted to drive. I was nervous since I hadn't had much driving experience because I had no car to practice with. I told her I was too nervous, but she just pulled over to the side of the road, got out, came around the passenger side, and opened the door. "Scoot over," she said. I got behind the wheel, and she told me everything to do. Fortunately, the car was an automatic. I drove from Eugene to Salem; I then pulled over to have her drive again. I'll never forget her and her kindness. I hope she is doing well today. That was also the weekend I decided if I ever made it to college, I would go to the University of Oregon.

Summer ended. Kristine was planning to move to Salem with a girlfriend, and I was about to start my senior year of high school. Kristine's parents felt it wouldn't be fun for me to continue to live with them since Kristine would be moving out at the end of the summer. Kristine's mom spoke to my grandparents, and they were happy to have me come live with them. So here I was back with Poppy and Grammer again. They didn't live out on the farm anymore. They had sold the farm years before and now lived in Stayton, just three few blocks from the high school. It was very convenient for me to just walk to school. As always, I enjoyed staying with them. They always made me feel at home. Even though they were older now and Poppy was retired, they I still had fun with them. We would tease each other all the time.

During my senior year, I continued to work for the school superintendent and for Mrs. Lavoy. I had been saving my money so I could go to the dentist. My parents never took me to the dentist because we were too poor, and I don't believe they ever thought about it. I knew I had a couple of cavities, and I wanted to have them fixed. I asked Mrs. Lavoy if she would take me to the dentist because it was too far for me to walk. She would drop me off and pick me up after each appointment. The dentist couldn't believe that I had never been to a dentist because I only had four cavities. He was also surprised when I told him I was going to pay the cost myself. I reassured him that I had the money in savings. I was thrilled to have my teeth fixed and cleaned. Mrs. Lavoy said she was very proud of me during that time as well.

My senior year went fast. I was as excited as all my friends to be graduating from high school. My dearest friends, Marge and Sharlene, were not planning to attend college, so we would talk about getting an apartment together. We planned to move to Salem where there were more jobs available. I was surprised they didn't want to go to college because I always thought if your parents could afford to help you go to college, why wouldn't you want to go? The only reason I didn't plan to go was that there would be no money from my poor parents. At this point in their life, neither one was working anymore. Dad received social security, and my mom received a pension from the Federal Government. I always figured I'd just get an office job and eventually get married like most of the girls in the small town of Stayton. In fact, when everyone was taking the college SATs, I was across the street working in the school superintendent's office. There didn't seem to be any reason for me to take the tests since I could never afford to attend college.

Toward the end of my senior year, I walked into Mrs. LaVoy's office to work for her during my free period. She stopped me at the door and told me to kneel-down. At that moment, I knew I was in trouble. I knew if I kneeled down on the floor, my skirt would not touch the floor. The school rule was your skirt had to touch the floor when you were on your knees. There were many girls in school who did not follow the rule. But I did what she asked and kneeled down in front of her. She said in a very stern voice, "Your skirt is too short." My response was, "Everyone else wears their skirts short." She immediately told me to walk home, change my clothes and report back to her. As I walked home to my grandparents, I was extremely angry with her for sending me home and embarrassed at having made her mad. At the same time, I dreaded going back to her office to face her again. I didn't want to hear a lecture, and I didn't see why my hemline couldn't be as short as the other girls at school. I kept pondering how I would react to her when I entered her office. I knew she would say something, but I didn't know what. As I walked into her office, she looked at me with a stern look on her face. She said, "Now, that's better." She then asked me to come over to her side of the desk where she was sitting. She took my hand, looked me in the eyes, and said in a gentle but somewhat stern voice, "You're not like everyone else, and don't you ever forget it!" I meekly mumbled, "OK," and proceeded to get to work. As I worked, I remember feeling love for her. I never forgot what she said. She, along with Irene Morey, the superintendent's wife, and district secretary, took care of me all the way through high school. They gave me the support and confidence I had never received before. They helped me to feel like I wasn't lower than other people because of being so poor and having parents who couldn't provide for me. I loved them both very much, and I wanted to make them proud of me. From that moment on, she was Mayme Lavoy to me, not Mrs. Lavoy.

Graduation was very memorable for me—and for others, I'm sure—but especially for me because of the three surprises I received. My grandparents attended as well as my sister and her husband, Allen. When my sister and her husband graduated two years earlier, I sat in the audience holding my nephew, Tony, who was just a small baby at that time. Both my sister and her husband were very popular when they were in school. Everyone was in awe that they continued to go to school and graduated together. The night of my graduation, I felt represented like everyone else even though my parents did not attend.

I walked down the procession with my friend Daren. When Daren and I were freshmen, we made a pact to walk together at graduation. Though we were friends, we did not spend time together socially. We hung out with different groups and rarely interacted outside of school. Daren was a little shy, and I was outgoing, and we just ran in different circles. We never forgot the pact we made four years earlier, and we were both excited to walk through graduation together.

Surprise number one was when the principal was calling out the names of students who qualified to receive an honorary certificate for maintaining a 3.5 or higher GPA throughout high school. I never paid any attention to what my GPA score was since I didn't believe I would ever go to college. To me it was not important. That night I heard my name called and I was in shock. I just sat still, and my classmates looked at me and motioned for me to get up. I heard my name called again, and I saw the principal looking at me with a smile on his face. This time I got up, walked down the platform, and received my certificate. When I returned to my seat, I also had a smile on my face and a feeling of considerable pride. I sat there thinking, *well what do you know, I made it to the upper level.* I didn't feel inferior anymore. I was in the elite group. Wow, did I feel great.

Surprise number two was when I received my diploma. One by

one, names were called, and my classmates would walk down off the platform to receive their diplomas. The diplomas were in a hardcover folder about the size of half a page. The folder was blue with our Eagle mascot embossed in gold on the cover. When I got to my seat, I opened the cover to look at my diploma. I didn't see my diploma. What I saw was a half-page handwritten note signed by Mayme LaVoy and Irene Morey. The note read, *we have a gift for you in the foyer on the gift table, so don't forget to look for it, Love Mayme and Irene.* I never expected to receive a gift just for graduating from high school—not from family members and certainly not from Mayme LaVoy or Irene Morey. I was fighting tears as I re-read the note over and over. This is another example of how they took care of me during my high school years. They wanted to make sure I had a gift like everyone else.

Surprise number three was what was under their note: a certificate stating I was the recipient of a scholarship that would be sent to me each year that I attended a university. The scholarship was $600 for each quarter of college. I just sat there in a daze as tears filled my eyes. I was overwhelmed, but at the same time, I kept thinking, *why would they get me a scholarship when they know I can't attend college?* I did not know the significance of this scholarship until several years later.

My gift turned out to be a beautiful coral colored knitted sweater shell. I loved the gift and hurried to find Mayme and Irene to give them hugs and kisses. Then I found the rest of my family and gave and received hugs and kisses from them. That was a night I will never forget.

Shortly after graduation, I moved into Salem to live with my sister and her husband Allen and their two little boys, Tony and Eric. I needed to find a job, and I knew I would have a better chance in Salem. There weren't any jobs in Stayton, and I really didn't want to live in Stayton anymore. It was lonely for me living with my grandparents now that I didn't see my friends every day. It was time to move on. My grandparents understood but said they would miss me. I helped my sister out by taking care of my nephews during the day while she and Allen worked. During this time, I was also looking for work. I was looking for administrative work in an office since that was the only work experience, I had.

I went to one interview at a company where they needed someone to file. The filing room was in the basement of the building. I was shown the area where I would be working then I was led into the office of the person interviewing. I sat down in front of a large desk with a middle-aged man sitting behind it, looking at me. He told me that he knew I could certainly do the work, but he didn't believe I would be happy. He said working in a basement filing was not what I should be doing. I thanked him and left. I was fortunate to soon become employed as a dental assistant for a dentist in Salem. I enjoyed the work and learned a great deal about negotiating, helping, and calming people. I eventually became interested in a career as a dental hygienist. I knew they made more money than dental assistants. This job didn't pay much, but I was so happy to be employed and felt so very independent.

As weeks went by, I saved my money so I could move into an apartment with my girlfriends as soon as they found jobs in Salem. I was also saving for a car. I took the bus to work every day. This added extra time to my workday. I would arrive about forty-five minutes early each morning and had to stay until about an hour after work ended to catch the bus home. Eventually, Marge and Sharlene found jobs in Salem, and we moved into a furnished apartment. We were so excited to finally be independent and to have a place of our own.

Living with my two best friends, Sharlene and Marge, was wonderful. Now I felt I was their equal and was not inferior. I made about the same amount of money they made. I wasn't the poor one anymore. The next year and a half went quickly. I finally saved up enough money to buy a car, but I still didn't have a driver's license because I didn't have a car to practice with. Marge, who had a car, suggested I practice with her car. When I wanted to get my license, I was eighteen years old. I borrowed Marge's car and headed to the Motor Vehicle Department. I passed the written portion without any problem and waited for the driving portion. I was so nervous having the instructor watch me that I went down a one-way street the wrong way; I made an illegal left-hand turn and did a terrible job at parallel parking. When we got back to the Motor Vehicle Department, the instructor pointed out my errors and said I did not pass the test. He told me to practice for a week and then come back. I immediately started crying and said I didn't have a car to practice with, but I did have enough money to buy my own car, and I could practice then. I must have caught him at a weak moment. He said he'd pass me if I promised to only drive to work and home for two full weeks after I purchased my car. I promised him I would, and he gave me my driver's license. The following Saturday, my brother-in-law, Allen, went with me to look for cars. I wound up buying a 1965 Ford Mustang Fastback. The exterior color was aqua, and the interior was white. I was so happy and proud. I had to admit that I was nervous driving. I kept my promise, and for two weeks, I only drove from home to work and back. After those two weeks, I felt much more comfortable driving, and then I drove everywhere.

During the time we were in the apartment, Marge moved to Portland with her boyfriend Dan, and Sharlene and I moved into a different apartment with another friend, Barbara. However, a short period of time later, Barbara was engaged to Gary, and soon, Charlene became engaged to Larry, and I broke up with my boyfriend, or rather, he broke up with me. I was devastated. I had spent an entire year being engaged to Terry while he was in Viet Nam and when he came home, he was changed. He had developed a very violent temper. He was very jealous as well. He accused me of cheating on him while he was deployed in Viet Nam. I never cheated, but he didn't believe me. After I got over my devastation, I was angry that I had waited a full year for him. I should have been having fun and going out on dates, but instead, I just patiently waited for him to come home. What a wasted year, I thought. Well, after pondering just what I was going to do with my life, I came up with a plan. I knew I didn't want to get married, but I felt that if I stayed in the Salem area, I would wind up getting married, and my life would be stifling.

One afternoon I called Mayme LaVoy and asked her if she could meet me after work. I told her I really needed to talk to her because I needed her help. We decided to meet in Salem in the lounge area of a large department store.

The two of us sat down on a couch. She asked me to tell her what was going on. I told her my boyfriend just broke up with me, and then I started crying. She asked me why I was crying. I replied, "I don't know." She immediately said, "Well, then stop." I quit crying, and she asked me what I wanted to do now. I told her that I wanted to go to college next fall. "Well, OK," she said, "we have work to do, so we better get started." I have my sister to thank for my determination to attend college. At this time in her life, she was divorced from Allen and with the help of student aid, she was attending a community college, working parttime and raising her two boys by herself. This gave me great confidence. If my sister could attend college, then I certainly could.

Mayme called after a couple of days and asked me to come by her office at the high school on Saturday so she could give me an application to fill out for college. She said I should fill out applications to more than one college to make sure I got into one of them, but I said the only college I want to attend was the University of Oregon. Since my GPA was above a 3.5, she reassured me I wouldn't have any trouble getting accepted. However, since I did not take the SAT while in high school, I'd have to schedule a time to do that. She signed me up to spend a Saturday taking the tests. Mayme also helped me fill out financial aid papers, and we mailed in all the required material, including my essay.

I asked my grandparents if I could move back in with them to help save money for college, and they were delighted to have me back. So, for the next nine months, I saved as much money as I could. I received notice that I was accepted to the University of Oregon, that I qualified for financial aid and was scheduled to work in the administration office on campus. Mayme reminded me of the scholarship she was holding for me. It was the $600 per quarter scholarship. She helped me find a place to live. I knew I was too old to live in a dorm with eighteen-year-old freshmen girls since I had been living on my own and was now almost twenty years old. She found a co-op that was originally a sorority. I applied and was accepted into a co-op of girls, so I had a place to live. My car was almost paid off, so I refinanced it to lower my payments. They were then low enough for me to handle with my modest income. I was all set.

The nine months went by quickly, and I was all scheduled to leave for Eugene. I needed to say good-by to Mayme and Irene before I left, so I called them and set a time to visit them on Saturday afternoon. I remember I had on a navy-blue A-line shirt, which came down just below my knees, a white sweater, and white flats. Both Mayme and

Irene commented on how well dressed I was and how mature I looked. They both smiled, and Mayme said, "Oh look, our little girl is all grown up now." I could tell they were so proud of me, and although I was a little scared to be going on this whole new venture in my life, I was extremely excited. I thanked them for everything they had done for me. They looked at me like proud mothers. We gave each other hugs and kisses, and I left to go home to my grandparents to start packing.

The next morning with my car full of all my belongings, I said goodbye to my grandparents and started my drive to Eugene. It seemed a little strange to be going off to college all by myself; however, I was twenty years old and not your typical high school graduate. The college was only a forty-five-minute drive away, but it seemed like a whole new life was opening up for me. I pulled up in front of the co-op and saw that other students were moving in, their parents helping. I parked and went in to check out the place.

The lobby and living room were large and lovely. I climbed the stairs to the bedrooms. The room was small. There were two desks, two chairs, two closets and two daybeds in our room. The restroom was down the hall, and the sleeping porch was at one end of the building. I really didn't like the idea of having to sleep on bunk beds on the sleeping porch, but we couldn't sleep in our rooms unless we were sick. I unloaded my car myself and picked out my side of the room since my roommate hadn't arrived. After I finished unpacking, I decided to take a walk across campus.

The walk made an impression in my mind that I've never forgotten. The sun was out; however, it was cold enough a coat was needed. I had on a pair of hip hugger jeans and clog shoes. As I walked along the sidewalks covered in brightly colored leaves of various shades of brown, yellow, green, red, and orange, I kicked them with my foot and thought, *I am so lucky to have finally made it to college.* It had been a long time since living in San Diego and thinking about college. There were many years I had forgotten the pledge I made to myself or had given up on the idea, believing I would never get the chance because my family was poor. I had never prepared for college other than keeping my GPA above a 3.5 in high school. I did this only because I was competitive and because school was where I could excel and be noticed and praised for my quality of work. When I was in school, I felt like everyone else. When I was home, I felt different, beneath everyone, poor and lonely. Now here I was in college, and I was like everyone else. Students came from all backgrounds. Some students had more money than others and wore better clothes, but a majority of the students lived in jeans and carried a backpack. I couldn't wait for registration and classes to start. I walked through campus, trying to familiarize myself with the location of the buildings. Campus seemed so large to me on that day.

That evening at the co-op, we had a meeting right after dinner, and different tasks were assigned to each student. We all had to share in the chores, particularly washing dishes. My first task was helping to wash the lunch dishes. I didn't mind having a chore; however, with my tight schedule, it was sometimes difficult to get back to the co-op between classes. I soon realized I was not contented living in the co-op. I had been on my own for so long that the other girls seemed young and immature to me. I didn't feel like I had anything in common with them. I really didn't like sleeping on the porches with all the other girls. At the end of the first week, I drove to my sister's apartment and spent the weekend with her and my two nephews. I felt lonely in the co-op and out of place with the immature girls. I drove back to Eugene on Sunday evening, determined to find another place to live. During my break on Monday morning, I walked to the student union and headed to the bulletin board at the back. There must have been five to ten 3 X 5 index cards pinned to the board under the category of "roommate wanted." I took all of them off the board and went back to the co-op. I went to my room and proceeded to start calling. I got to the third card when someone on the other end sounded nice, and the apartment sounded nice, and even more important, the rent was about the same as what I was paying in the co-op. I walked over to the apartment, only a few blocks away, and met the two girls living in the two-bedroom apartment. One bedroom was large with enough space for two people. They shared this bedroom. The other was smaller, but it had a large closet and a sink with a counter. This was to be my bedroom. We made an agreement; I paid them my portion of the rent and then went back to the co-op to pack up my belongings.

I was so happy to be in an apartment again since this is what I was used to. I had my own bedroom that I really liked. I could go in there, close the door and study. One of my roommates was a student at the university, and this was her senior year. The other girl worked. They were both twenty-one years old. That made them just slightly older than me. It felt so good to be with mature girls again.

The remainder of my college years was filled with similar issues, experiences, and problems as other college students. Running to classes, cramming for tests, spending hours in the library doing research and writing papers. Not to mention boyfriend problems, broken hearts, keg parties, looking forward to the quarter ending so there would be a break and then looking forward to the term starting up again. Time went fast for me. When I wasn't in class, I was working at the administrative office on campus. I did receive financial aid, but I needed to work to supplement my income. I didn't mind. In fact, I enjoyed working in the administration office, where I made new friends. The main difference between my friends who did not work and me was when I was at the office working, they were sleeping. We all studied at night. I just had to drink more coffee to be able to stay awake. The other difference is that they partied more than I did. Their parents were paying for their college, and I was paying for mine. This made a big difference. I took it a little more seriously than they did.

There were a few situations and experiences that stand out in my mind. I'll never forget the two blind students I tutored one quarter during my sophomore year. This was a community service program under a community health class I was taking. I had options of what I could do. Tutoring blind students sounded interesting. I drove to the community health center and waited for the two students to show up. Soon, in walked a girl and a boy, each one carrying a white cane and both juniors in high school. I said hello to them and introduced myself. They were very friendly and said hello and introduced themselves. This was a room they were familiar with since they used it the prior quarter with another tutor. I would read to them, and they would take notes in braille. Soon they were trying to teach me to read braille. I let them touch my face so they could get a sense of how I looked. They both had a great sense of humor, and our lessons during that quarter were filled with laughter and continual teasing. I admired them and had a lot of respect for them. I couldn't imagine what it would be like to be blind. I learned patience and persistence from them that quarter, and I hope I helped them learn something they could carry with them in life.

Since I had decided I wanted to become a dental hygienist, I was required to register for a majority of the science classes that were offered. One quarter I had to learn the skeletal system and the circulatory and muscular systems. Learning the skeletal system turned out to be easy because the class had two skeletons to look at, and that made it easier to memorize. Working with a skeleton was fun. I finished the skeletal portion without any problem and received an A on the final exam. Learning the circulatory and muscular systems, on the other hand, started out as a disaster. The professor announced we would have to study in the labs on real cadavers. I didn't know what a cadaver was and when the instructor explained, I knew I didn't want to touch them. Instructors would be available to help us, but I wasn't sure that would help me much. When I walked into the lab the first time and saw the cadavers, I immediately turned around and walked out. I decided I would not be going in there again. There was no way I was going to touch and feel dead people cut open and exposed. The labs reeked of formaldehyde, and it was disgusting to say the least. During the next class meeting, the professor expressed the importance of studying with cadavers. He said if we didn't study with the cadavers, we wouldn't be able to pass the class. *Okay*, I said to myself. *I'll really try.* I arrived at the science lab that evening and walked in. I put on my rubber gloves and walked around, looking at the four or five cadavers in the room. I then turned around and headed for the door. The professor's aide followed me out and stopped me in the hallway. I was almost in tears. "You have to get over this," he said. "If you don't study from these cadavers, you won't pass the class. "What bothers you the most," he asked.

First, I said, they should be buried. They must have family someplace, and I can't believe their family would want students pawing over them and calling them nicknames, like "Rosie the prostitute." He explained that these people either donated their bodies to research, or no one claimed them when they died, so their bodies were given to the university for research. He also explained that the reason they give funny names to the cadavers is to help the students. You need to keep your sense of humor, he said, or you won't be able to manage studying with the cadavers. After he said he'd walk around with me for a while and help me get started, I agreed to go back in. After a couple of weeks, I couldn't even smell the formaldehyde in the room. I did notice my books smelled of formaldehyde, but I didn't mind. I received an "A" in the class and was so happy that I would never have to study from cadavers again. However, I knew that if I had to, I could.

One of my classmates, Marnie, wanted to become a dental hygienist as well. After our sophomore year, we were required to take a test in Portland where the dental school portion of the University of Oregon was located. My boyfriend was a student at Washington State University, and his family lived in Lake Oswego. He was going to be home the same weekend we were scheduled to take our test in Portland. We decided he would find a date for my friend Marnie, and we would go out the Friday night we were up in Portland. She and I arrived early in the afternoon and visited campus. We didn't like the feel of it because it wasn't like the University of Oregon campus in Eugene. We talked about whether we would like to live in Portland, away from all our friends and in the middle of the city. I remember we were extremely disappointed. We went back to our hotel and waited for my boyfriend and his friend to show up. The four of us went out on the town. We had dinner, drank beer, played pool and stayed out late partying. We both were very tired and not feeling very well the next morning. We had headaches and were in no shape to take an exam. Somehow, we managed to make it through all the testing, but we both knew we flunked the tests. As we drove back to Eugene, we were so excited because we knew we weren't going to move to Portland; we were going to stay in Eugene. Sure enough, we both received letters stating we did not get accepted into the dental school.

Another experience I remember is about one of my dear friends, Tony. I met Tony sometime during my junior year of college, and we became friends. There was a three-day weekend coming up, and Tony suggested we drive to San Francisco. Tony's nationality is Italian, but he was born and raised in San Francisco. His mother still lived there, and he wanted to see her as well as have a short vacation. He didn't have a car, so I offered to drive if he would show me around San Francisco.

We left early in the morning on a Friday and drove straight through, arriving in San Francisco sometime in the evening. Tony's mother was such a sweet woman. She was so happy to see Tony. She fixed us dinner and visited with us for a while. That night Tony said he would sleep on the couch, and I could sleep in his old bedroom. I agreed, but only if he agreed to trade places the next night. We had a full day on Saturday. This was my first time in San Francisco so Tony took me all over so I could take in all the sights. We rode the cable car, walked the wharf, and I, of course, I wanted to see Haight Ashbury. I was a little disappointed that I didn't see any flower children dancing around and hippies sitting on doorsteps. Later in the afternoon, we went back to Tony's home to have dinner with his mom and plan the evening. We headed out that evening to hit a couple of Tony's favorite bars and clubs and listened to jazz music. It was a most memorable weekend. I'll never forget Tony or his sweet mother.

An experience that changed my life was when I met my husband-to-be during my senior year. It was early spring. I remember being concerned about what I was going to do when I graduated. My close friends said they were going to move back home then start job searching. I didn't have a home to move back to, so I was concerned; no, I was worried. One day, one of my track friends, Mark, asked me to walk to Susan Campbell Hall with him because he needed to speak to his counselor. I agreed to go with him since I needed to check in with my advisor whose office was in the same building. I was beginning to fill out all the necessary paperwork for graduation, including job searches, and I would meet with my advisor each week. Mark showed me where I could meet him when I finished. After meeting with my advisor, I walked to the office Mark indicated he'd be in. I walked into the office and behind the desk where Mark was sitting was the counselor for student athletes, Ulysses. I said hello and told Mark I had to get going, but he could stay if he wanted to. Mark stayed; I said goodbye to Ulysses and left. A week or so later, Ulysses stopped me as I was walking along campus heading to work and asked me if I would like a ride. He was driving a white Nissan 240Z, which I thought looked cool. I hesitated but then agreed, and we chatted as he drove me across campus to my destination. About a week later, he called and asked me out on a date. Since I already had plans to go out with my girlfriends,

I said I couldn't and explained why. He said he was impressed that I didn't call my girlfriends and cancel. He continued to pursue me and after a couple of weeks, we went out on a date. We became friends, and eventually, our friendship developed into a relationship. Before the end of the spring quarter, we were living together. When I graduated from college, we were talking about marriage.

.

High School Graduation

June of 1967

High School Graduation

# IV
## "My Friend Pre"

It's been twenty-plus years since Steve Prefontaine's fatal automobile accident in Eugene, Oregon. Not only are people still talking about him, but they also made a movie about him, actually two movies. The first one is out now and playing at the local theater. It's titled *Steve Prefontaine*. As I sit in the theater waiting for the movie to begin, I start reminiscing.

It was the spring quarter, 1969, and I was sitting in my English writing class at the University of Oregon waiting for the bell to ring. I loved coming to this class this morning. Not that I was particularly thrilled with the content of the class, but I loved the building in which class was held, and it was a beautiful sunny morning. The classroom was on the second floor of Deady Hall, one of the older buildings on the University of Oregon campus. The building was completed in 1987 and was named after Matthew Deady. He was a judge of the Territorial Supreme Court from 1858 through 1859 and then became the US District Judge for Oregon. The exterior walls were a mixture of stone and brick splashed with tall windows framed in the ivy that grew all over the building. Parts of the building were completely smothered in ivy. The first time I walked into the building during winter quarter I felt a presence around me—as if the spirits of the thousands of students who walked the halls, sat behind the old desks, listened to lectures, and took notes over the years before me were somehow in the walls and throughout the structure of the building. I felt overwhelmed and honored to be a part of the knowledge that filled the air. I felt that energy again this morning. I was sitting at a desk that faced the door. I looked up from my notebook just as he walked into the room. "Oh my God he is so cute," I said to myself. He had a serious look on his face, and his medium brown hair laced with blond streaks was combed back except for the strands of hair that fell down slightly over the top of his eyes that were wide and beautiful. My eyes moved around the room, then back to him. *I'd like to get a chance to meet him*, I thought.

The classroom was small. One entire wall was lined with tall windows and this morning, the early spring sunlight was streaming in. I had my back to the windows and my eyes on the classroom door and the student standing in the doorway. The desks were arranged in a horseshoe shape around the perimeter of the room. There was a podium in the front of the blackboard that filled one end of the room. The professor smiled at the student and said, "Congratulations on your impressive performance Saturday." He looked toward the professor, smiled, and said, "Thank you." Then his eyes moved around the room, looking for an empty desk. I sat there wondering what that conversation was about and what he was being congratulated for. He caught me staring at him, and he smiled at me. I smiled back. He started to walk around the back of the desks. There were empty desks scattered around the room. He passed several of them and kept walking toward me. *Oh my God, is he going to sit next to me?* I wondered with excitement. He reached the seat next to me, sat down, turned to me and said, "Hi, I'm Steve." I responded, "Hi Steve, I'm Gloria." From time to time, he would ask me a question, and after I responded, I would ask him a question. I found out he was from Coos Bay, Oregon, a small town by the coast. He laughed when I told him I was from a small town in Oregon called Stayton. "Stayton, where the hell is Stayton?" he asked. I laughed. "It's not as much of a hick town as Coos Bay," I answered, "and it's not far from here." He told me he was a freshman. My heart sank. *Well, he's too young for me,* I thought. I was interested in older guys, at least older than me. I was twenty going on twenty-one, and he was barely nineteen. When we stood up to walk out of class together, I thought, well, he's definitely not my type because I like taller guys. Besides, someone that good-looking is bound to have a girlfriend. We walked through campus together, talking, until I had to head in another direction for my next class. We said goodbye, and he headed off to the Student Union, or SU as we often called it. He was in search of one of his track friends since he had a break between classes. That's how our friendship started. Class met on Monday, Wednesday, and Friday, and we continued to sit together each day. That is, each class day that he showed up. He would miss class regularly, especially on Mondays or Fridays. On a weekly occasion, the professor would congratulate Steve for something he had done over the weekend. I still had no idea what it could be. I was too embarrassed to ask Steve. I thought, now here's a fellow student who must be skilled at something associated with the University of Oregon, and I should know what it is, but I don't. I sat there looking at him, wondering what he could be so skilled at. He didn't look like a jock, so what else could it be? He certainly didn't look like a football player, and he was too short to be a basketball player. I had no idea, but I wasn't about to ask him. That would be too embarrassing for me. I felt like I was probably the only one in the room; heck, I was probably the only one at the whole University, for that matter, who didn't know who he was. Well, I wasn't going to let him know that I didn't have a clue, but I was determined to find out.

One Monday after class, another Monday without Steve attending, I decided to walk to the Student Union to get a coke since my next class wasn't meeting that day. As I headed for an empty table by the window, I walked past a table filled with newspapers. I saw a familiar face staring up at me from the front page of the paper. It was Steve, "Steve Prefontaine." I sat down, picked up the paper and read the article. Now I know what Steve did over the weekends to cause the professor to congratulate him. He ran track. More than that, he broke old track records and set new ones with his running. "Oh, my God, he's Oregon's track star," I almost said out loud. I was both impressed and excited. I sat there thinking, *He's got to be the most popular guy on campus. He can have anyone he wants for a friend, and he chose me.* I felt honored. I felt special.

The following Wednesday, Steve came to class. I decided we were good enough friends by now that I could share my secret with him. After class, as we were walking to the Student Union, I told him that I really didn't know who he was until I saw his picture and article in the paper that prior Monday. He was extremely surprised and asked me why I hadn't told him before. I explained that I was too embarrassed because I felt like I was the only person on campus who didn't know who he was. He looked at me with a smile on his face and said, "Really." He laughed as he gave me a big hug. He seemed to be so pleased with my secret. I didn't know why. From that time on, I began to give Steve a tough time about missing class. After I'd congratulate him on his achievement during the track meet the prior weekend, I'd say, "So what, so you had to attend a track meet; that's no excuse for missing class on Monday." "Poor baby, you have it so rough." "I work fifteen hours a week, carry a fifteen-hour class load, and never miss a class." He'd just laugh at me. That was the way our friendship developed. I'd try to put things back into perspective. I enjoyed teasing him as much as he enjoyed my teasing. I took the role of being his big sister.

The quarter ended, and that was our first and last class together. From time to time, he would stop in the business office on campus where I worked to say hello. He would visit with me for a brief time, or he would call me up on the phone and we'd talk for a few minutes, but mostly he would just drop by my apartment unannounced. When I opened the door, he'd have that big grin on his face. I think he did that because he liked seeing the surprised look on my face. He would usually be restless and wouldn't stay long. He always had something to do or someplace to be. Our visits were short, but they were filled with tenderness and concern for one another.

I enjoyed being around Steve in public because Steve never went anywhere without causing a stir. Girls were always falling over each other to get his attention, and the guys were just as bad in their effort to say something cool about the time records he set, or how he ran his last race. I used to say things like, "Oh my God, Steve, they act like you're something special. Don't they know you're just a spoiled little country boy from the hick town of Coos Bay who misses class all the time but happens to be able to run fast." He'd laugh at me. "You're just jealous." We could always make each other laugh.

The first time he came into the business office to see me, he caused quite a commotion. I was busy at my typewriter when I heard someone say, "She's over there." I looked up, and there was Steve, grinning at me with that little boy grin of his from across the room. There was no place for us to visit with everyone gawking at Steve, so I took a break and walked outside with him. We chatted before he was soon on his way. When I walked back to the office, the students and university employees who were working in the office at the time came up to me, excitement on their faces. Someone said, "I didn't know you knew Pre." "Yes, we're friends," I said. Another student who also worked in the business office said, "He's so cool and so good looking." One of the guys standing near spoke up, "Do you realize what a great runner he is?" I said, "Well, of course, I do; after all, he is my friend." I walked back to my desk feeling privileged and perhaps a little taller. *No wonder Steve likes all the attention he gets; it's fun and it makes you feel special.* I also remember thinking about how stupid all those girls were for wanting to be Steve's girlfriend. As much as Steve's first reputation was "Track Star," his second was "Heart Breaker." I once told him, "Steve, I'm so glad you're not my boyfriend." He responded, "Why?" with a puzzled look on his face. "For one thing, Steve, you can't be trusted," I said. "Rumor has it that you chase after every blonde-haired girl you see, and fortunately, my hair is brown. You'd break my heart, Steve, and then I'd never want to see you again. So being friends is so much better. We'll always be good friends." I got a great big grin out of him as well as a hug for my comments. "You're something else," he said.

When I first arrived at the University of Oregon, I knew nothing about track, and I didn't know anyone who was in track. After meeting Steve, he introduced me to a couple of his teammates, and I became friends with a couple of them. During the times I didn't see Steve, my other track friends would fill me in on the latest news. I remember hearing about the time Steve jumped off the edge of the balcony into a swimming pool and cut his foot. This was during a pool party attended by the track coach and part of the track team. I heard his teammates were mad at him. They thought it was a very stupid stunt done only for attention without regard for the consequences. Later, I read about him setting another track record while running with a tennis shoe filled with blood from a cut that hadn't healed yet. *Boy,* I thought. *Steve sure played that one for all it was worth, didn't he?*

The school quarters came and went quickly, and Steve and I would always say good-bye for the summer. I would always leave for Salem, Oregon, where I worked in a dental office throughout the summer, and Steve would go off traveling to various track meets, working on his running skills and his dark tan. However, my junior summer I stayed in Eugene to attend summer school. This was my chance to gain a couple extra credits so that I'd be eligible to graduate in June of the following year. Summer school turned out to be easier and more laidback than the regular school sessions. I was able to arrange my schedule to have a couple of afternoons free each week. This was the first time I had that much free time. I used it wisely, "sunbathing." I either headed out to the reservoir to swim and water ski with friends or sunbathed in my front yard. I decided this was my chance to get a darker tan than Steve. He would always show off his tan in front of me every fall when we were back in school. I was planning to outdo him this time.

It was the summer of 1972. The Summer Olympics were being held in Munich. Everyone knows what happened in Munich on the 5th of September—the Palestinian terrorists took eleven members of the Israeli Olympic Team hostage and ended up killing the athletes. The loss and the grief were terrible. But Steve gave us a feeling of pride. We were proud to be Americans. My face was glued to the television, like every other Oregon student. I was so thrilled watching Steve race in Munich. I cried when he came in fourth, but at the same time, I was proud of him. I knew he was affected by the terrorists' attack, and this affected his race; however, he ran his heart out like always. You cannot ask for anything more than that. He had nothing to be ashamed of, but I could feel the pain he must have been going through at the end of the race. I knew it would be tough for him. I did not get a chance to see Steve again until sometime after the Olympics, and he didn't want to talk about what had happened, so I didn't push him.

In early May of 1973, my track friend, Gary, called me up and invited me to go with him to the dual track meet between University of Oregon and Oregon State held in Corvallis on May 5th. I remember Gary saying, "You've never seen Pre run a race in person, so I thought you might like to go." I was excited to go, and I told him so. With my hectic schedule, I very rarely was available for sports events. My girlfriends weren't interested, and I didn't want to go by myself, so I usually would not go. I had known Gary for several years, and he had become an exceptionally good friend of mine. I always enjoyed our time together. Gary informed me that Oregon State did not have any significant runners that year, so Gary and his Oregon teammates choose not to participate in this meet. Steve was scheduled to run in the three-mile race, and I was excited to watch and to spend time with Gary, whom I hadn't seen in a while. I remember being so happy that day. It was an exceptionally warm day for early spring. I had on a lime green sundress that I usually only wore in the summer. I had not seen Gary since his twenty-first birthday back in March, and we were planning to stop for a beer after the track meet. I was looking forward to that since he was finally old enough to go into a bar and have a drink with me. I was twenty-three at that time. The track meet was, as I recall, not very crowded with spectators. I remember seeing Steve standing on the edge of the track before the race. He looked up in our direction because our group was so noisy. He spotted me and said, "Hi Gloria," and waved to me. I yelled, "Hi!" back. It seemed like the race was over very quickly. We all yelled for Steve during the entire race. It was easy for him that day. He came in first for the three-mile race. After the race, he came by to chat for a minute. He was so surprised and happy to see me at the track meet and made a point of saying this was the first track meet that I ever attended. I could tell he was pleased. It was the first and last time I ever saw Steve race in person.

I will never forget the last time Steve came over to my house. It was just a couple of weeks after the track meet, on an early Saturday morning. The sun was shining, the sky was blue, and the air, though crisp, felt like the beginning of summer. My roommate, Peggy, had just left to go jogging for the first time. Peggy was what I would call a real bookworm. She always had her nose in a book studying. She could sit for hours with a cup of coffee on one side of her and an ashtray filled with cigarette butts on the other, with her book and note papers sprawled out all around her. She was so determined to get through college with straight A's. I used to beg her to go out partying with me, or go shopping, or just go goof around, but she would say she had to study. "Peggy," I'd say, "You're going to graduate with a four-point, and no one is going to care. I'm going to get a better job than you because I'm getting a more rounded education." I'd say, "There's more to an education than what's in those books." Or I'd say, "Don't you know employers only want to know that you were smart enough to graduate, not what your grades were?" It didn't matter to her. She had to achieve A's. Occasionally I'd get her to go out with me. I never knew if she finally said yes because she really wanted to go just got tired of me begging her. Once we were out, she would lighten up, and we'd have a fun time. She was fun to be with. She had a profound sense of humor.

Peggy's skin was very pale but very beautiful. Her face reminded me of the face of a porcelain doll with flawless pale skin, big eyes with long lashes and long straight hair. I would tell her that she needed to come outside with me and get some sun on her face, but she always refused. I couldn't even get her to go for a walk with me unless it was to class or to the library to study or do research.

So, when she came into the living room one morning dressed in gray sweatpants, jogging shoes and a big sweatshirt and announced she was going running, I was shocked. "Peggy," I said in laughter, "you're going jobbing! I don't believe it!" She said she wanted to lose a couple of pounds and get into shape. I wished her luck, and off she went. I headed for the kitchen for another cup of coffee. I was in no hurry to start my Saturday, and I didn't feel like studying yet; that would come later in the day. I settled down in a big over-stuffed chair we had in the living room of our duplex. Peggy and I moved there the beginning of our junior year. We had to get out of the large house we shared with five other students. Too much partying went on all the time. There was never a quiet time to study unless you wanted to get up at five in the morning. It was always quiet then, but Peggy and I were always too tired. One winter during winter break, the basement flooded, and that's when Peggy and I decided we needed to start finding a place to move to since we both shared the basement.

Well, anyway, I was drinking my coffee, listening to the stereo, and looking out the window at the hawthorn tree coming into bloom when I heard a knock at the door. I headed for the door, thinking Peggy must have made it for a mile or less, ran out of breath, came crawling back and was standing on the porch too exhausted to open the door. I swung open the door, and there was Steve. He had a more mature look about him now. His mustache contributed to that. He had that same look on his face as when he first smiled at me four years earlier. We gave each other our usual bear hug greeting. He said he wanted to thank me for coming to the track meet in Corvallis. "That's the first time you've ever watched me race in person," he said softly. "Yes," I said, "and I wish I had attended all the other track meets held at Oregon because it was very thrilling to watch you run. Now I understand why you have such a following." He came in, and we sat on the couch. After we talked for a while, each one taking turns filling in the other one with what had been happening in our lives, I looked at him and said, "Now, Steve, don't get mad, but they're talking about you again." One minute he says, "Fuck 'um, I don't care what they say." The next thing he says is, "Now, what are they bitching about?" Since I had other friends who were members of the Oregon track team, I was often well informed as to what Steve was doing and what people were saying about him. I would often enlighten him as to the latest gossip. Usually, we would just laugh about the latest rumors. This time it was different. "You're hogging the limelight." I told him. "Why do you have to come across as being so arrogant and such a hard ass?" "Oh, I'm tired of their whining," he said in an irritated voice. "If they want some of the glory, they should work as hard as I do and break their own records." "Steve, they are never going to be as good as you," I said, "and they're never going to work as hard as you because they are not as obsessed with winning as you are. It's time to get rid of that chip on your shoulders, don't you think?" "You don't know what you're talking about," he said to me. He was pissed at this point. "Oh, yes, I do!" I said, "They're your teammates. They're not putting you down or just merely talking about you behind your back because of jealousy. Steve, all I'm saying is shine in your own glory, but don't take away theirs. You don't have to prove anything anymore; no one's laughing at you now. No one's saying you are too small to be a fast runner. You're there, you're at the top, and it's time to soften a little." His response was, "I'm not going to let what people say change how I act. I'm out there to win races." He was irritated with what I was saying. "Steve, I'm telling you this because I care about you and your teammates care about you," I said. "It won't hurt your race to share the limelight, and it just might make you feel better. You say you don't care what people say about you, but I do. I know you don't do it to hurt them, but that's what ends up happening, and you know how that feels." A grin appeared on his face, and he looked up at me. "Just try, Steve," I said. "Don't come out on the field when a race is finished and one of your teammates won until the crowd stops cheering for them. "OK," he said but not very convincingly. "Steve, you should be so proud of what you've accomplished. Do you realize people will be talking about you for years to come? You'll be remembered for all the records you set and for the years you've spent here at Oregon. We'll be graduating at the end of this year, and no one will remember I was ever here." Steve reached over and squeezed my hand as he said, "I'll always remember you. I don't know anyone like you, Gloria. You've put yourself through college. I mean, you did it all by yourself, no help from your parents. I don't know anyone else who's done that. Most guys I know couldn't do that. Your days start at eight every morning and end at five every afternoon. You're either in class or at work, and you still manage to get good grades. I'm not going to be graduating at the end of this year because I am behind in credits. I think what you've accomplished is pretty amazing. On top of that, you've got a great body and you're good looking," he said with a laugh. "But most important to me, you like me for me, not for my running. You were my friend before you knew who I was, remember?" "Yea," I said, "I remember." "Well," he said, "I think you're the one who's pretty remarkable. I'm proud of you, and I'll always remember you," he said as he reached over and hugged me.

Just then, the door flew open, Peggy stumbled in, gasping for air. sweat dripping down her face as she fell into the stuffed chair I was sitting in earlier. Steve and I just stared at her. I was trying awfully hard not to laugh. "Peggy, are you alright?" I asked. She nodded her head up and down while she was still gasping for air. As soon as she caught her breath a little, I said, "Peggy, this is my friend Steve." "Hi," she said, and he said hi. "This is Peggy's first day of getting into shape, and she decided to start out jogging," I said as I grinned at Steve. "In case you couldn't tell," I added. "Say, Peggy, Steve knows a little bit about running; maybe he can give you some pointers," I announced as I poked Steve in the arm. "Sure," he said. "You might try starting out a little slower and work your way up to a full run. Jog a couple of blocks, then walk a couple of blocks, then jog a couple of blocks, on and off like that until you build up your stamina. Otherwise, you'll burn yourself out." She thanked him for the advice as she stumbled off to the bathroom to take a shower. Steve and I sat there grinning at each other.

We sat on the couch and talked for a while He then stood up, saying he had to get going. I walked him to the door, and we walked outside onto the porch. We gave each other another hug goodbye and told each other to take care. As he walked down the steps, I said, "Now be nice." He just grinned at me. As he got into his orange MGB convertible sports car, I hollered out, "Steve!" He turned around as he said, "Yea?" "Slow down, I hear you're driving too fast." He laughed, waved goodbye and drove away. I stood on the porch watching as his car turned the corner. I stood there a short while before going back inside.

Peggy came into the living room where I was now sitting. "Where's Steve?" she asked. "Oh, he had to leave," I replied and added, "Say, Peggy, do you know who he was?" "Yea, he was your friend Steve." "Yea, but do you know who he really is?" I replied. "That was Steve Prefontaine," I said. I watched Peggy's large eyes become even larger and then fill with anger. A frown formed on her lips. "No!" she said in a loud voice. "Yes," I said, nodding. "Oh, my God, how could you do that to me. I'm so embarrassed. He knows everything there is to know about running, and you said he knew a little bit. Oh my God!" she repeated, "How could you do that to me!" "Peggy, calm down," I said. "We weren't making fun of you, and Steve really was trying to help. If you had known who he was while he was here, you would have been even more embarrassed." "Well, I guess you're right," she said, "but still just the same, I could just die!"

I picked up the newspaper early one morning, and there he was again plastered on the front page. Two years had passed since I last spoke to Steve. We both went through our different changes, with school, boyfriends, girlfriends, graduation, life in general. I was married and working not too far from the University. Steve was still in Eugene. I never saw him, but of course, he was still running his races. I and everyone else in Eugene were expecting to read about the track meet that had taken place over the weekend with the visiting athletes from the Finnish National Team. This time as I read the headline, I wasn't feeling pride as I always had in the past. There was a pain in my stomach that made me feel like I was going to be sick. My neighbor from across the street, Paul, who knew Steve was a friend of mine, came over early that morning to tell me the news about Steve before I read it in the paper. Paul and his wife, Twila, had heard the news over the radio. As soon as I looked at his picture, I remembered the first time I saw him on the front page, and my eyes began to fill with tears. Soon they were streaming down my face. "Oh, my God, No!" I said as I tried to read the words through my tears. "No, I can't believe this." I sat on the couch with the paper on my lap, staring at the picture of Steve. The tears turned to sobs. I thought softly to myself, *Steve, I told you to slow down. Damn it, Steve, why didn't you just slow down? Why did you have to drink before you got into that damn sports car that night? Why did the party have to be up on that dangerous road? Why did I have to lose such a dear friend, why?*

I didn't go to the memorial services held at Hayward Field on that sad Sunday. I couldn't; I was in too much pain. I just couldn't see myself sitting in the stands while the Hurst was driven around the track with Steve's body inside. It would have been too painful for me. I mourned in silence, by myself. I heard later that afternoon that as the hearse went past everyone in the stands, they all yelled, "Go Pre, Go Pre." I couldn't have withstood that. Steve would understand why I wasn't there. Oregon lost a track star; the US lost a potential gold medal winner, but I lost a dear friend.

Twenty-plus years and a lifetime later, I'm sitting in a dark movie theater. My twenty-year-old son, Marcellus, is sitting next to me and Crystal is on the other side of him. The movie we're watching is not a movie my son would have gone to see on his own. The Steve Prefontaine movie had just hit the theaters, and I wanted to see it. After all these years, the pain was still there. I couldn't go by myself. When the movie preview was shown on TV, I told my son and daughter I wanted to see the movie because Steve had been my friend in college. "No way!" was their response. I have proof, I told them. They weren't sure they believed me until, after searching through my boxes of memorabilia, I pulled out a postcard from Steve. The picture on the dingy yellow postcard was of the city of Cali in Columbia. Steve was there for a track meet our sophomore summer. On the card, he talks about the great tan he was getting. I had to laugh while remembering I beat him at tanning one summer. That was Steve, full of himself. He wrote that if he didn't make it over to see me during the summer, he'd see me back at school in the fall. Fortunately, he signed the card, Steve Prefontaine. It's the proof I needed for my kids to believe that he was indeed my friend.

I'm staring at the big screen now. In the movie, they are talking about how they saw a change come over Steve toward the end. How he seemed to soften a little. He began to step back and let the other track members receive their applause instead of rushing out onto the field to claim the attention of his fans. I'm sitting and wondering is it possible that I had some influence over Steve? Could be, or perhaps he was just maturing all on his own and at his own pace. No, I want to believe he listened to me that day in college and eventually changed. The movie is about over, and I'm glad the room is dark as my eyes are filled with tears. One or two tears spill out and run down my face. I can see my son out of the corner of my eye. He's looking at me and has a look of concern and love on his face. I whisper softly to myself as I watch the Hurst move slowly around Hayward Field, "Go Pre, go Pre."

Florence & Me my Junior Year of
College at U of O

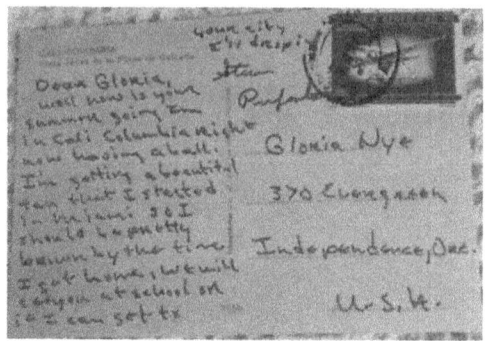

Post Card from Steve Prefontaine

The first I met Ulysses in his office

Birthday Party for Ulysses
[The night he hit me]

Graduation Day for Ulysses Received his PhD
[I'm pregnant with Marcellus]

# V
## "Broken Marriage #1"

As mentioned earlier, Ulysses and I were living together the last quarter of my senior year of college. When I graduated, he was close to being finished working on his PhD while also employed full-time by the University as counselor for student athletes. I was happy. Ulysses was working hard on his dissertation, and I was working in an office while I was waiting to get a teaching position within the City of Eugene. At that time, you needed three years of experience before the Eugene school district will hire you. I felt like I finally had a home and was no longer worried. His position at the University allowed us to attend parties held by faculty and other acquaintances of his. I thought if we married, our marriage and life would be great. After a few months, I noticed Ulysses was drinking more often to the point of being a mean drunk. I saw the red flag but chose to ignore it since everyone drank in those days. Then one night, I threw him a birthday party for about twenty people. One of the individuals attending was an old girlfriend of his. I could tell she still cared for him, and while we were talking, she mentioned she was thinking of moving to California to further her studies in law. I encouraged her to go and not wait around to see if Ulysses and I were going to break up. I told her we loved each other and were eventually going to get married.

Later that evening, when the party ended and everyone left, Ulysses became extremely angry with me. I believe he was upset because I was talking to his ex-girlfriend. He didn't like that. His anger scared me, and I was afraid he would hit me, so I went next door to use our neighbor's telephone. It was late, but three girls lived there, and I knew they would be up. One of our guests was Ulysses' doctorial mentor and a professor of psychology at the University. He and his wife had attended the party, and I wanted to call them to get advice as to what I should do. Saul, his mentor, answered the phone, and I explained the situation. He said to go back home and just talk with Ulysses, and everything would be all right. He said Ulysses just had a little too much to drink.

Ulysses was still mad when I went home, but I ignored him and got ready for bed. I figured he just needed to sleep off the alcohol. He came to bed shortly after and started arguing with me. I told him I didn't want to argue, but he kept on, and finally, I couldn't take any more of his ranting, so I got up and started to leave the bedroom. The next thing he did was jump out of bed, turn me around, and sock me in the face with his closed fist. He hit me so hard I fell backwards and passed out just before I hit the floor. When I came to I was dizzy and could see blood everywhere. He grabbed a towel to try to clean up the blood. He gave me a small towel to hold on my face because I had blood all over my face. He picked me up and put me in bed, got into bed himself and kept saying he was so sorry. He soon fell asleep or perhaps passed out. I became very still. I was traumatized. When I woke up early the next morning, my face and head hurt so badly. I reached up and felt my face. It was swollen, so I got up and slowly made my way to the bathroom to look in the mirror. I couldn't believe what I saw. My right eye was swollen almost shut and was very bruised. My cheek and mouth were extremely swollen. I cleaned off the dried blood, brushed my teeth as best as I could, got dressed and then woke Ulysses up to tell him to take me to the emergency room at the hospital. He was noticeably quiet and nervous as he drove me to the hospital.

After the doctor reviewed my x-ray, he informed me the bone under my left eye was fractured in three places, with bone fragments floating in the area. He said I needed surgery to wire up the bone after the swelling went down. As strange as it may seem, I was embarrassed at what had happened to me. I told the doctor how it happened because he asked me. The doctor did not make a report to the police. Doctors weren't required to report domestic violence at that time. I had to wait a week for the swelling to go down, and during that week, I went to work. Because of my embarrassment, I made up a story about being in a car accident even though it looked like someone gave me a black eye. I was just too embarrassed to tell them the truth.

A week later, when I was in the hospital waiting for surgery, Saul and his wife, Fran, came to visit me. Saul was deeply sorry for not really listening to me when I called him that night. He left to get ice cream and probably to give Fran a chance to talk to me. While he was gone, Fran shared her feelings with me. She told me I should not marry Ulysses because he would always feel that he was beneath me. Our marriage would never work out because he was Black, and I was Caucasian. I appreciated what she had to say, but I didn't believe her. I had always prided myself on not being a racist, unlike some of the people in the small towns I grew up in. I didn't believe we would have any racial problems. The truth was, our problems were not racial; they were much worse, but I wouldn't learn that until years later.

About a week after I returned home, my friend Tony came by to visit me. I was so embarrassed for him and his girlfriend to see me. At that time, I thought I was embarrassed for Ulysses, but now I realize I was embarrassed for myself because I stayed with him. Yes, he was abusive, but wasn't I stupid for staying with him?

Ulysses was truly kind and nice to me for months after the violent accident, so I finally believed my worries were over. I envisioned us having a good life partly because he would be a licensed psychologist making good money and I would be a teacher, so between the two of us, we should want for nothing, and we should have a happy life together.

Shortly after my surgery healed and all signs of my prior trauma were gone, I received a call from my college advisor saying he had a teaching job for me at a high school in Elmira. Elmira is a small size town west of Eugene; it takes about a half-hour to get there. It is really like another world. Most of the students came from lower-income families, but they were all nice. I taught the freshman classes in Science, Health and Drivers Education. Since this was the first year the high school had a freshman class, I had nothing prepared for me. Every test, every hand-out, and every overhead slide had to be prepared by me. I felt like I was a chapter ahead of the students. Well, I actually was. My science classes were terrible from my perspective because my experiments often didn't turn out quite right. Fortunately, after the second quarter, they removed me from science and asked me to teach the driver education class, though not the actual driving portion. I was not too thrilled with teaching driver education, but I figured it had to be better than science. Classes started out fairly slow, and I felt my classes were boring. That's when I contacted the Motor Vehicle Department in Eugene and arranged for them to give the written tests in my classroom. Soon my class became extremely popular, and everyone who was fifteen years old and did not have a driving permit signed up for my class. If they wanted an "A" in my class, they had to pass my tests and pass the state driver's permit test. There were students who lacked transportation to Eugene, where the nearest Motor Vehicle Department was located. They were so excited to be able to pass my class and also get their learning permit.

The year was overwhelming with all the extra work and hours I had to put in for each class. By June, I was burned out and was relieved when the principal told me they were putting the freshmen back in middle school because they didn't believe they were mature enough for high school. There would be no job for me the following year— that was fine with me. My high school teaching career lasted only one year, but because of that year, I have a deep admiration for teachers. Imagine trying to teach a classroom of thirty students with different personalities, different emotional levels and problems. There were students who were hungry and also angry. Teaching students is no easy task, but highly rewarding when students come up to you to say thank you at the end of the school year.

Ulysses and I were married during the year I taught at the high school. The evening of our wedding was a real unhappy experience for me. I chose to forgo a honeymoon and use our money to purchase the house we were living in. We held the reception at our house, and it was a wonderful party. However, after everyone left, Ulysses passed out in bed. I sat in a chair in the living room and began to think about our marriage as tears ran down my face. I finally admitted to myself that Ulysses had a drinking problem. A bride is not supposed to be sitting alone in the dark because her new husband is passed out. I thought about my parents and my alcoholic father. When he was drunk, he was mean, and he physically abused my mother. This happened often when I was a child. At that moment, I decided things would be different with my marriage. I thought that once Ulysses realized I really did love him, he would feel more confident about me, and he wouldn't drink so much. Well, I was young, only twenty-three years old, and obviously very naive.

Fast-forward thirteen years. We have two children, Marcellus and Crystal. Marcellus would be eleven and Crystal would be five. The years were filled with many episodes of alcoholic crisis, increased debts, poor credit, financial strain, arguments, car accidents, DUI's, just to name a few. Throughout our thirteen years of marriage there were good times, but they were rare. By this point, Ulysses was abusing more than alcohol, and he was socializing with individuals who were taking and dealing drugs. I finally reached a turning point when I realized I needed to take care of my children and remove them from this harmful environment. Even then, I hesitated to leave. Fortunately, I was working for a company making good money, and I felt secure. I knew Ulysses would make it hard for me to leave, and I knew he would start pestering me at work. I was through with the years of struggling financially when we shouldn't have been. I was tired of Ulysses' increased alcoholism and his womanizing.

Ulysses was rarely around, and when he was, he was either drunk or recuperating on the couch from a week of drinking. He had a private practice as a licensed psychologist and was always away from home. He had a contract with the professional basketball team counseling the athletes who were abusing alcohol or drugs until he wound up getting a DUI. His contract was canceled soon after.

As Ulysses' alcoholism and other addictions proceeded to get worse, as well as his angry behavior, I got healthier. He was beginning to hang around people who were dealing and taking street drugs. This was the turning point for me. I knew I had to get our children out of this situation. I wanted to make their home safe, and to do this, I knew I had to leave their father. I'll never forget the time he came home late one night and went directly to his office, which was just off the main entrance of the front door and called me in to help him. I walked into a briefcase full of money staring me in the face. You need to help me count this money, he said. I was in shock and asked where he got the money. He had talked to a drug dealer into investing in his practice and the small office building we owned. I was immediately terrified. I knew he would not use the money to promote his practice or the leasing of our office building. I was afraid the individuals who loaned him the money would eventually cause harm to him, our children, or me if, the money wasn't paid back. I told him to take the money back. I shared my fear with him, but as usual, he tried to make me believe I was being foolish. We counted the money, and he took the $30,000 to the bank and deposited it. I don't know where the money went because I never saw any of it. During this time, Ulysses was wearing three-piece suits with French cuff shirts and was driving a jaguar. He had to look the part of a doctor, so he said. I was driving an old Datsun station wagon, and I would load it up each Saturday with dirty clothes as I headed to the laundromat because I didn't have a washer and dryer at home.

Within that year, we had to move because we didn't qualify for a mortgage. We were trying to buy the house we had been living in for two years. We had an option- to-purchase agreement, but Ulysses squandered all our money, and we had to move. We moved into a condo not too far from where we were currently living. Several months had passed, and I could see that Ulysses was drinking increasingly more. I believe he was also using other drugs. He was socializing with one of his clients who were addicts. I finally accepted the fact that he was not going to get better, and I knew I needed to move out with our children so I could provide a safe environment for them. I remember the night I made the decision. I was lying in bed; it was late at night. The children were asleep, and Ulysses was out. As I lay there thinking about leaving and feeling great fear, I asked myself this simple question. "What would be the worst thing that could happen if I left?" The first thing that came to my mind was, *what if I'm happy and I have no one to take care of, what will I do?* That thought shocked me into realizing I had to leave. I finally realized I was so emotionally scarred that I couldn't even think about taking care of myself. That was a turning point for me. I was becoming just as sick as Ulysses. I was finally ready to make the move to safety and freedom. Most important – safety for my children.

When I told Ulysses, "I'm leaving and filing for a divorce," he became very depressed and distraught. He asked me to see a counselor with him. I knew it was too late since I was already mentally gone, but I agreed to go. I told him to find a counselor and make an appointment, and I would go. We drove in separate cars and arrived about the same time for the appointment. After me telling the counselor that Ulysses was an alcoholic, a womanizer, and he was both verbally and physically abusive to me during our thirteen years of marriage, the counselor looked at Ulysses and asked if this was true. Ulysses said it was. The counselor replied all of this behavior had to come to a dead stop if he expected to save our marriage. Ulysses said he was willing to do that. The counselor told Ulysses that he should know better since he also was a licensed psychologist. I told the counselor that I had already emotionally left; it was just a matter of me finding a place to move into, and then I would be leaving and filing for a divorce. I said I had waited thirteen years and he had only gotten worse, and I was concerned for our children. I told the counselor there was no more that I could say, and no one was going to change my mind. The counselor looked at Ulysses and said, "It's too late." He looked at me and said I could leave if I was ready. I got up, thanked the counselor, then left. Ulysses stayed and continued to talk with the counselor.

The kids and I moved to an apartment a month later. Ulysses would not make it easy for me to relocate, that I knew. I had no extra money for the moving costs plus deposit and rent on an apartment. I calculated I needed an additional $1,000 before I could move. Ulysses said if I was going to move, he wasn't going to help. I had to do it all on my own. After fretting and worrying about how I was going to come up with the money, I called a prior employer and asked for his help. At first, he asked if there was someone else I could ask for help, and I said if there was, I wouldn't be calling him. He asked me to come to his office the next day. He was hesitant about giving me the money because he wasn't sure how I would pay him back. I told him I didn't know how either but that I would definitely pay him back. He gave me a check for $1,000, and the next week the children and I moved into our new apartment. I tried to make it as pleasant for them as I could. Crystal was only four; she took it the hardest. Marcellus was happier about the move. Being the eldest, he had bad memories of his dad and how he acted when he would come home after a night of drinking.

We got all moved in and set up our new home with new rules. Every night just before bedtime, the children would climb in bed with me, and we would watch a program on television. I'd have a child on each side of me, and I would cuddle with them while we watched television. I continued to reassure them everything would be all right and they were safe now. I told them no one would ever hurt them in our new home. The children soon adjusted and seemed to be relaxed and happy. I told them the three of us had to work together to make this new apartment our home. I made a list of chores and assigned specific ones to the kids and to me. We became a team working together, we were happy, and we felt safe.

I can still vividly remember a dream I had during this time. I was driving a car late in the evening; it was very dark outside. There were people in the back seat, and who they were kept changing. I was driving in the forest, and I could hear the growls and howls of lions, tigers, and wolves. It seemed they were coming toward me. I was so scared as I drove the car, hoping to find a safe place to hide from the scary animals and voices. Every now and then, I would look in the back seat to find someone new sitting back there. Finally, I saw a small castle in the distance and headed in that direction, hoping to arrive before the animals. I pulled up in front and ran to the exceptionally large door. I quickly opened the door and, once inside, slammed it shut. I ran up the winding stairs to the very top and walked over to the window to look outside. I was searching for the animals while I said to myself, "Who will take care of me?" I heard a voice say, "I will take care of you." As I turned around to see where the voice was coming from, the room became bright with light, music started playing, and I said to myself, "Oh, I will take care of me just like I always have!" Instantly I felt at peace and woke up.

However, the children's father continued to be agitated. He harassed me both at home and at work. He would call me at work three or four times a day. My boss was incredibly open minded about understanding my situation, and he had the receptionist screen my calls. She always told Ulysses I was in a meeting. He finally stopped calling me at work. We were able to relax and become calm, and most important, our home was safe and without anger.

A couple of months after we moved into our apartment, I received a call from the individual who loaned me the $1,000. He said he needed help with the accounting on the apartment buildings of which he owned a percentage. I worked for him part-time in the evenings and on weekends. Soon, my debt was paid off, and I was putting money into savings. I will always be grateful to him for his help.

The children didn't always like spending weekends and blocks of time during the summer months with their father. They said it was boring and there wasn't much for them to do. Marcellus was about thirteen when he finally told his dad he wasn't going to spend time at his home anymore. Ulysses became terribly angry and came to my home to drag Marcellus out. Marcellus had a friend visiting us, and I told him to call the police. When Ulysses heard me, he jabbed me in the chest and said he would kill me. Then he got into his car and drove away. The police showed up and asked us to tell them exactly what happened. When we explained the situation, the police said there was nothing they could do because he had the right to drag Marcellus out of the house since it was his weekend to have the children. He said they could only arrest him if he assaulted me. I was in shock. I told him Ulysses didn't assault me, but he did jab me in the chest and say he'd kill me. The officer said if I wrote that down and signed it, they could arrest him. I didn't want to do this, but I made a promise to the children they would be safe in my home, and I wanted Marcellus to know that his father couldn't come into our home and drag him out. I explained everything to Marcellus and told him I was going to sign the document.

He said he thought I should sign. The police left and said they would bring Crystal home to me since she was at her father's house. When the police brought her home, she was truly angry when she came in and didn't want to talk to me for a while. It was extremely hard for her to understand why the police took her father. This was the last physical incident we ever experienced with Ulysses. Years later, when Crystal got older, she too announced one day that she wouldn't be spending weekends with her father anymore. He was able to accept this without making a fuss.

# VI
## "Single Mother"

Shortly after the children and I moved into our new apartment, I met a wonderful man at a Christmas Eve party. My children were also there. It was an incredibly special and exciting party complete with Santa handing out presents to all the children. This was so much different from our past Christmas Eves, when the children and I would spend the evening together, and Ulysses would be out drinking. Soon after, we began dating and eventually fell in love. My children loved him, and he also loved my children. Rick was his name, and he was so good and loving to the children and me. Unfortunately, we met too soon after my broken marriage. Months after we started dating, he asked me to marry him. I broke his heart when I said, "I feel like I just got out of prison, and you are now asking me go to jail." He was a patient man and said he would give me time. We dated on and off for approximately six years. Whenever I felt he was coming close to asking me to marry him, I would push him away. When we were together, he took us on vacation trips; he spent time playing with the kids, and he spent having dinners and family time with us. He attended as many of Marcellus's baseball games and Crystal's softball games as he could. He loved to cheer them on. When we went out of town for my son's baseball tournaments, he was there. We could always count on him. When we were apart, I would miss him and find myself wishing I could move past what was blocking me from saying yes to his marriage proposal. It was always fear that would lead to anxiety. I would find myself thinking it just wasn't meant to be. I thought I wouldn't be feeling anxiety if we were meant to be together. That's what I would tell myself. He would often tell me he had enough love for both of us. I would tell him I loved him, but I was just so stuck. When we were not together, it was because I would feel so guilty, I'd tell him to stop waiting for me. I'd tell him to date other people because it made me feel so bad that I couldn't make him happy. When we were together, we had so much fun. We had so much admiration and respect for each other. After a while, he would get brave and ask me to marry him. I would become filled with anxiety and eventually push him away. Those were years of turmoil. I took full responsibility for causing so much internal pain for us both.

It had been a year since I last saw Rick. During this time, I spent time working on my inner fears. The anxiety was gone, and I felt that I was ready to commit to him if he still wanted me. I called him one afternoon and asked him to come over because I had something to share with him. He was in shock when I told him I had finally overcome my fears of marriage and that I could now fully commit to him. I expressed my love for him and asked him how he felt. I could see the pain in his eyes when he expressed how so often he had longed to hear my words but had finally given up. He explained he was dating someone now. I asked him if he was in love with this woman. He said he wasn't. I believe deep down inside he was, but as he looked at me, he was very conflicted. I told him then it wasn't too late; I would wait for him to decide. He said it was complicated, and he had a lot to think about.

The months passed. Occasionally he would call or stop by for a quick visit. I could see he was in turmoil, so I would tell him I had patience for him. One of the last times, I became so distraught I couldn't stop crying. I realized he had decided not to be with me. I told him I loved him and that I forgave him, and he left.

Months passed with no contact. Then, during one of Crystal's softball games, I looked up to see Rick walking toward me. It was so good to see him, and I felt happy about feeling so much love for him yet just keeping it to myself. We visited for a while, and he helped me work my video camera, so I'd have good videos of Crystal. We gave each other a big hug, and he left. Weeks later, I learned he was getting married, and a couple of months after that, I learned he was battling cancer. He passed away that year. As I reflect, I know he came to tell me goodbye that day at the ballpark. My children and I will never forget him and will never stop loving him.

The children flourished in school and became regularly active in sports. I began working toward a master's degree in business through City University in Bellevue, Washington. It took me about two and a half years to finish the MBA program. I took evening classes since I was working full time. Often, I would take my studies to either my son's baseball game or my daughter's softball game, and parents would seem amazed that I was able to work full-time, raise my two children, attend all their sports activities, and also work toward my master's degree. I remember telling them I had more free time now because I didn't have to take care of their demanding father.

The years I spent raising my children as a single mom were some of the best years of my life. I had so much fun with them, and we were remarkably close. I enjoyed each phase of their lives, and I was so happy to not be living in fear all the time. I developed self-confidence and was happy. I didn't worry as much as I used to; however, fear and anxiety have always been a part of my life. I developed a powerful anxiety trait as a young child, and I never overcame this stifling affliction. We didn't have much money, but I was able to provide very well for my children. They never felt deprived and never went hungry. I made sure we remained in the same community so they wouldn't have to change schools or make new friends in a new town. The three of us had our own home responsibilities, and they were good about doing their chores. We were what I'd like to think of as a reasonably normal family. Allowances were given and taken away, and punishment was meted out depending upon the situation.

Marcellus could sometimes try my patience. One time he ran away from home. He was mad at me about something, and I had sent him to his room. He was twelve or thirteen years old and had a mind of his own. I walked into his room later that night and found him gone. He left a note on his bed that said something like he ran away to stay with his friend Dennis because he couldn't talk to me. Dennis lived just over on the next block. I couldn't help but smile when I read the note. I called and asked to speak to Marcellus. When he answered, I said, "Marcellus, if there's one thing you have that perhaps some of your friends don't have is a mother that you can talk to who will listen and who is fair." He responded, "I know." He said he was sorry he'd run away, and could he stay for just a little while longer, then he would come home. As the years went by, Marcellus would bring a friend home every so often who was having trouble with his family, and he'd ask if his friend could stay with us. I always said, "Yes," but first, his friend had to call his parents and tell them where he was. I also remember Marcellus would say to a new friend he brought home, "Talk to my mom and look at her when you do, and she will like you." He'd also told his friends to "never lie to my mom because I don't know how she does it, but she always knows when someone lies." One time a friend of his stayed with us for a month or two before he decided to go back home. He came from a very wealthy family and was living with his father and stepmother. Our home was simple and small, and I was surprised that he would want to stay with us in such a tiny little bedroom until one day he said, "You know what's missing from my home that you have a lot of here?" I replied, "No, I don't know; what do we have?" He said, "Love, and there's a lot of it here."

To say that Marcellus was a handful would be putting it lightly. As much as he was a joy, he was equally troublesome as he was growing up. He didn't much like school except for the social aspect of it. When he was in junior high, he began to get into trouble by not obeying the school rules. His grades were slipping. I reached a point where I needed to see a change. I took him in for a psychological evaluation. I told the psychologist I wanted to find out if there was a problem with depression, attention deficit or another condition we needed to address or was my son just spoiled. After running him through a battery of tests and evaluations, the psychologist determined he was depressed because of the hole he had dug himself into at school. So, my attitude changed after that. I became even more firm with him. Weeks later, he came home and told me he got kicked out of school. I asked him what he was going to do about that since he needed to be in school. He said he wanted to go to a different junior high and that he would call his dad since he knew the principal at that school. I just told him not to look to me for help because I was finished bailing him out of trouble. Well, his dad scheduled an appointment to meet with the junior high principal. I had to attend this meeting along with Marcellus. At the meeting, the principal explained the basic school rules to Marcellus, including attending all classes and getting good grades. She explained that there would be no excuses and that this was his last chance. If he messed up at her school only once, he was out. He agreed to all the rules, got himself back into junior high and graduated from that school.

High school was a repeat of junior high. He kept his grades good enough to be eligible to play baseball. He loved baseball, and he was an incredibly talented player. During the summer, he played on the Kirkland All-Star Baseball team each year.

I can't remember how often I went to the school to talk with the principal about my son because his grades were slipping, or he was in trouble of one thing or another. If there was any trouble going on at school, my son was always on the fringe of it. I was impressed that he had a reputation with the entire faculty at the school for being honest. It was like, if you really wanted to know what was going on or who started what, just ask Marcellus. He'll tell you the truth.

He got kicked out once. The only way to get him back in was to meet with the school board, the principal, and the vice-principal. The reason given for kicking him out for the remainder of the quarter was he headed to the restroom without a hall pass and ran into the vice-principal. During the meeting, I waited for Ulysses to say something, but he just sat there looking as if Marcellus deserved to be kicked out. I became like a mother bear fighting for her cub. At the hearing, I was able to show that the vice-principal was having a bad day, he took it out on Marcellus, and he used Marcellus' past infractions against him. Marcellus was back in school the following day.

Early one Friday evening—Marcellus was a sophomore in high school—as he was waiting to get picked up by his friends, he told me they were planning to grab the construction barricades and place them around the car of one of their female friends. He said the girls put Oreo cookies on their car; this was their way of getting even. It was all in fun. I told him not to take the barricades because that was stealing. He said they were just going to borrow them, and they would take them back after they saw the girls' reaction when they couldn't move their car. Again, I told him not to do that. I said the owner of the construction company wouldn't think it was funny. His friends came and off they went.

It must have been about midnight when the phone rang and woke me up. When the caller identified himself as an officer from the Kirkland Police Department, I immediately said, "They didn't take those barricades, did they?" The officer asked, "You knew about this?" I explained the whole prank to the officer and made sure he knew that the boys were only borrowing the barricades for their prank. He said I could come down to the station and pick up my son.

One evening I was at the grade school attending a school fair. This was Crystal's last year there, as she would be entering junior high the following school year. A police officer that I knew came up to me to say that the owner of the construction company was not going to press charges against the boys. The owner retrieved the barricades, and when he was told the whole story, he thought it was a good prank and dropped the charges.

I was relieved and told Marcellus about my conversation. I suggested he tell all his friends involved in the escapade. The next day I received a call from one of the parents inquiring if it was true the construction owner dropped all charges. After I confirmed, I was told the family had paid an attorney a retainer to represent the case. They were happy to get their retainer back. I was not worried because I didn't believe the construction owner would press charges after he heard the story, especially since I could attest it was meant as a prank. I knew several officers at the Police Department, as I met them when Marcellus was in junior high school. I purchased a black Raiders jacket for him. He told me all the kids had them and they were popular. He came home one day and told me the police stopped him while he was walking along the street with his friends and took his jacket. I was upset, partly because I paid good money for that jacket and partly because I thought they might have singled him out because he was Black. I immediately called the Police Department and made an appointment the next day with the chief of police. I let him know I was not happy about them taking my son's coat that I had bought for him. The Chief of Police told me that gangs were moving into the area and were wearing this type of jacket. He didn't want Marcellus to be mistaken for a gang member. That made sense, and I thanked him for looking after my son. From that time on until Marcellus was out of high school, one of the police officers that I knew would come by and let me know that they were keeping an eye on Marcellus and that he was a good kid, and I didn't need to worry about him.

There was one frightening incident in Seattle that I will never forget. It happened when Marcellus was a senior in high school. I don't believe he will ever forget the incident as it was horrific. Rave dance parties were extremely popular at that time. They were held in warehouses in different areas of Seattle. There were drugs of all kinds at these dances. Anything to increase the intensity of the music and the experience would be used. One Friday night Crystal's girlfriend and her mother were visiting us, and Marcellus was out with his friends. The ten o'clock news came on the television, and there was a news flash about a shooting and killing at a rave dance in Seattle. I knew Marcellus was at that rave dance, and I knew he would be close to the incident because he was always on the fringe of trouble. Marcellus did not have a cell phone, so I began calling the friends whose cell numbers I had. I left messages because I was not able to reach anyone. No one called me back that night. Marcellus did not come home, and I didn't get sleep well that night.

The next morning, after I figured it was late enough in the morning for a teenager to be up. I called one of his female friends who hadn't returned my call the night before. I told her I was worried about Marcellus and asked her to call around and find out where he was and if he was all right. I asked her if she could please ask Marcellus to call me. Within an hour, he called. Not only had he been at the scene, but he was sitting next to the young man who was shot. They were sitting on the sidewalk just outside of the rave dance. The bullet just missed Marcellus, and he saw the young man's brains splattered. The shooter was on drugs that made him think he was in a movie, and he kept telling the young man he had just shot to get up. Then he ran with the gun into the dance. As soon as they heard sirens, Marcellus and the friends he was with ran for their vehicles and left as fast as they could. They stopped only to throw up. They went to a friend's apartment and sat up all night talking about what had happened. They were scared. They thought they would be arrested and end up in jail because they saw what happened and ran away instead of staying at the scene. I told him to come home, and we would call the police. He could tell his side of the story to the police from home. As it turned out, the shooter pleaded guilty, and Marcellus and his friends did not have to get involved. The whole incident bothered Marcellus enough that he lost interest in rave dances. I never liked them, so this relieved my worry.

Marcellus became lost after high school. I believe part of the reason was the lack of interest, support, and time from his father. He turned to alcohol and drugs like as did some of his friends; however, Marcellus was an alcoholic and couldn't stop. During this time, he received two DUI's, and because he ignored the court requirements, he wound up in the court system for years before he was finally free of the courts and of alcohol. He checked himself into a local treatment center for thirty days, and shortly after getting out, he completely stopped drinking. As of this writing, he has been alcohol-free for five years or more. He behaves as if he is lost. He has no direction and drive to succeed at anything. I stop worrying about and have just learned to keep my emotions in check and to love him from a far. I tell myself he is doing the best he can do at this point.

Marcellus was a good teacher for Crystal. She saw all the trouble he got into and all the problems he had and decided she would do things entirely different. She had close friends, was a good student, and never got into trouble. Or perhaps she was simply good at keeping it from me. Well, she did get into trouble once that I remember. When she and her friends were in junior high, it became popular to steal from department stores then brag about what they took. This had nothing to do with money since they all earned good weekly allowances; it was just a popular thing to do.

I received a call from the mother of a friend of Crystal's who was caught stealing. She named all the girls involved in stealing. I sat Crystal down and asked her if she had stolen anything from a department store. She admitted to stealing a sweater when she was shopping with her friends. I asked her to bring the sweater to me, and I was shocked because not only was the sweater very unattractive, but she also had the money to pay for it. After we had a long discussion, I called the department store and made an appointment for Crystal to meet with the store manager the next day. Crystal was extremely nervous when we walked into the store manager's office. She explained to the manager what she had done. She said she was sorry and would never steal again. She said she didn't want the sweater and gave it back to the store manager. The store manager gave her a lecture and told her what would happen if she stole again and got caught. She mentioned Crystal's friends; they were no longer allowed to enter the store without a parent. Crystal broke down in tears, said she was sorry and promised she would never steal again. She thanked the store manager, and that is the first and last time she ever got into trouble that I know of.

Crystal was highly active in softball, both in school and in the community. She went to all the school dances, and I enjoyed shopping for the perfect dress for her. She had her set of friends, and I do believe she enjoyed her school years. To me she enjoyed her high school years as well. I didn't find out until Crystal told me years later that she threw parties on the weekends I was out of town. I was so surprised. When Marcellus was in high school, he would come home from parties and tell me I never had to worry about him giving parties at our home because the houses always got trashed. He told me about spilt alcohol on the carpet and furniture and cigarette butts' ground into the carpet. He didn't want our home to get trashed, and he also knew I couldn't afford to pay for all the damage. I never worried about parties at our home. When Crystal was in college, the subject came up. Her parties were highly organized. She would stand at the door with her hand out for money to pay for the alcohol and to check the individuals trying to get in. If she hadn't invited them, she wouldn't let them in. She would have her girlfriends spend the night, and the next morning they cleaned the whole house before they went home. I never knew because there was never a sign of a party. By the time she told me, I congratulated her on throwing such organized parties and for doing such a decent job in cleaning up.

From Crystal, I learned parents should be incredibly careful what they say to their children, as we can leave lasting negative impressions. When the children were in grade school, I went on all their field trips. One time we were coming back from a field trip to the Ballard Locks. I was sitting next to Crystal on the bus when she looked at me and asked, "Mom, how come I don't look like you?" In my joking fashion, I blurted out, "Oh honey, I was going to wait until you were older to tell you that you were adopted." She immediately began to sob. I felt so bad for saying that. Not a very smart thing to say, and I don't know why I thought she wouldn't know I was just kidding. I calmed her down, explained it was a bad joke and apologized profusely. To this day, she has never forgotten that incident. It doesn't trouble her, but she does remind me from time to time it was a bad joke.

It's probably true Marcellus received more attention from me than Crystal because she always strived to be perfect. I didn't have to wake her up three and four times each morning because she used her alarm clock. I didn't have to get on her about doing her homework because she completed it as soon as she got home from school. This was not the case with her brother. I didn't mean to show more attention to Marcellus, but he was a handful. It was so nice to have one child who didn't cause me worry nor require so much of my attention. I realize I should have given her praise more often to balance the time spent between the two. I always told my children I loved them and showed my love equally, just differently.

During Crystal's junior year of high school, she turned sixteen and was ready to get her driver's license. Remembering I did not have a car to drive until I was eighteen when I purchased my own car, I wanted to provide cars for my kids when they turned sixteen. I remember how it felt to not have a car until I saved for one after high school. I was excited to purchase a car for Marcellus since his father would not or could not. Marcellus and his father were not talking during this time. I let Marcellus do the research to find the car he wanted. I just told him to keep it within a certain amount of money. He found an older Jetta Volkswagen in Seattle. I drove him to the dealership, and we purchased the car. He was so excited to get into the car and drive home. When Crystal was nearing sixteen, her father kept telling her he was going to buy her a car for her sixteenth birthday. He took her to car dealerships looking at cars. She was so excited and told her friends about her birthday present coming up. About a week and a half before her birthday, I received a call from her father asking me if I was going to buy Crystal a car. I told him, "No, I'm not. Crystal tells me you are." There was a long pause on the phone, then he said, "I don't have the funds or credit to be able to buy her a car; therefore, you'll have to." I was angry with him for making a promise he could not fulfill. I felt devasted after that phone call, but that was nothing compared to how Crystal felt. I knew I had to figure out a way to buy her a car. Marcellus had a friend who had a car for sale, and Crystal loved the car. It was a 300ZX Nissan. It was in excellent condition and was beautiful. The color was pearl white, and it was an automatic. I told her about the car, and she was excited, so I drew out money from my 401K and bought the car for her. She received the car just in time for her birthday. I was elated to be able to help my children with their first cars, and I felt sad for their father. He never experienced that good feeling.

Me & Marcellus on vacation in at
Disneyland, he's 3 years old

Me & Crystal in Hawaii, she's
seven years old

Crystal & Ballet

Marcellus & Baseball

Crystal & Marcellus

Crystal, Marcellus & Their
Father on Vacation

Receiving my MBA

My Proud Children

# VII
## "Broken Marriage #2"

By the year 2000, Marcellus was out of the house and working. Crystal would be graduating from high school in June. I had been working for Tom Bernard for six years at his industrial park. I was also supporting his family in non-financial ways. It started when his father-in-law was being treated for cancer. When Tom and his wife, Jackie, were traveling through Europe, I took Jackie's father to his chemo treatments. Jackie called me from Europe to ask that I send her special items she couldn't get in Europe. She was also battling cancer. Later, when Jackie was in the hospital, I'd visit her, and she would often call me from her hospital bed. She would be depressed, and I would try to make her feel better. Sometimes she just wanted someone to listen to her while she cried. Jackie's father passed away, and within a year after Jackie too passed away. I then helped take care of her mother, Simone. I often received telephone calls from Tom's adopted son, Jamie, asking for help or advice. He was sixteen and battling with his father. He was also struggling with the loss of his mother. When he got into a fight with his father, which was often, he would call me for help. I would pick him up and take him home or to school. It had been over a year since Jackie had passed away when Tom and I began dating. I didn't want to at first because I felt guilty since I was so close to Jackie. Tom soon convinced me Jackie wanted him to marry again, and she told him to find someone like me. After that, Tom swept me off my feet. He appeared to like my two children, and he offered to pay for Crystal's college. He helped to pay off my car loan and took me on trips to Europe, Thailand and wonderful places in the United States. Money was no object, and he wanted to pay for a huge wedding held at the Seattle Tennis Club. I felt like a princess and here I was fifty years old. I felt like I finally found my prince.

Tom surprised me with a planned trip to Europe. He wanted to take Crystal and Jamie; it would be a family vacation. This was the summer before Crystal started her senior year at high school. We went to London, Paris, Aix en Provence in France, and Spain. He planned the entire trip, including where we would stay and how long we would be in each place. I didn't realize that he hadn't planned any time for relaxing, which is important for teenagers. I knew Crystal needed to have time alone doing what she wanted, and I predicted Jamie would have the same desire. I also knew Crystal and Jamie would not want to see all the museums Tom had picked out, and actually I didn't want to see all of them either. I told Tom I wanted to find a place for us to stay when we arrived in Spain, and he was fine with that. I knew he would be tired and would need beach downtime for resting. I found us a modest hotel in the beautiful town of Tossa de Mar along the marvelous Costa Brava on the northeast coastline of Spain.

There was arguing and bickering in London and again in Paris. One time we were sitting outside finishing lunch. Tom was being bushy about what we were going to do next, and both Crystal and Jamie were disagreeing with him. Tom became agitated with Crystal, and she became very emotional. She began crying and got up quickly and walked away. Jamie looked at his father and said, "Dad, there's no reason to get angry; we're on vacation, and we should be having fun." I got up and went after Crystal. I calmed her down. I told her I wasn't going to let Tom ruin our vacation. I assured her, she and I would start doing things differently than what Tom dictated, if we wanted. When we went back to the table, Jamie announced he wanted to go skateboarding instead of going to a museum. Crystal and I announced we would go shopping, and we would meet up later. When we did tour a museum, I told Crystal she could walk around by herself and wait outside when she was finished looking through the museum. Jamie would merely walk around like he was half asleep and not look at anything. I tried to explain to Tom that I didn't want to look at ancient Greece artifacts or other country's artifacts while in Paris. I wanted to take in the beautiful places in Paris. Much to my surprise, Tom would walk through the museum at an amazingly fast pace, so we never had to stay too long inside any of the museums.

We had four days left on our trip when we arrived in Tossa de Mar. This is the place we planned to stay while touring Spain and particularly Barcelona. Tom wanted to stay in Barcelona, but I said he had to compromise we could stay in Tossa de Mar because I wanted to spend time on the beach, and I knew Crystal felt the same way. "What's a vacation without beach time?" was what I presented to him. He finally agreed. We arrived late in the afternoon, and Crystal was so excited she had a room of her own and didn't have to share a room with Jamie like she did in London and Paris. She was eager to have her own space and quiet time. During dinner that night, Tom announced we would be leaving early in the morning for Barcelona. He had the day all planned full of museums and other sights. He was not happy when I told him Crystal and I chose to spend the day at the beach, and we would not be going. Jamie said nothing, so Tom proceeded to tell Jamie what they would be seeing. It was around 10:30 p.m., and I fell into bed very tired. Tom began arguing with me that I should go with him to Barcelona the next morning. I stood my ground and told him I wanted to stay in Tossa de Mar and play on the beach with Crystal and that I was not going to change my mind. I was so exhausted and frustrated with him. I'd never seen anyone display this type of behavior. The more I told him to stop bothering me the more he pestered me. I told him I was tired, I wanted to sleep, and I wanted to rest on the beach the next couple of days. Tom persisted until 2:00 a.m., which is when he finally fell asleep. He managed to get up early the next morning and left with Jamie.

Crystal came to my room around 11:30 a.m. We made plans to get a bite to eat then hit the beach. We sunbathed, swam, and napped on the beach the larger part of the afternoon. It was so relaxing, and we thoroughly enjoyed ourselves. During dinner that evening, we took turns sharing our experiences of the day. Tom and Jamie's day sounded very hectic. They took in lots of museums and did a lot of walking. Jamie finally said, "Dad, I'm going to stay on the beach with Crystal and Gloria tomorrow." To my amazement, Tom just said, "OK."

The next morning Crystal and I headed for the beach and staked out our place. We were enjoying the sun when Jamie arrived and took his place alongside us. Sometime later, Tom arrived with his large camera and passport pouch hanging around his neck. It was quite a sight to see. He immediately opened up an umbrella and lounge chair and made himself comfortable in the shade with all his belongings. I headed for the water, which was very warm, and called for Jamie and Crystal to join me. We played around in the water for a little while. I called for Tom to join us. Jamie said, "Dad won't come into the water." "Why?" I asked. "He just won't," said Jamie. Crystal said, "I'll go up and tell him I'll watch all his stuff while he swims with you guys." Soon Tom was in the water swimming with Jamie, and they stayed in the water for a couple of hours. They rented a paddleboat and explored the shoreline. Later that evening Jamie quietly said to me, "That's the most fun I have ever had with Dad." I felt both sad and happy for him and was so glad we made the decision to hang out on the beach.

After we were back home, Tom mentioned that he wanted us to have a prenuptial, and I was fine with that. I believed he should leave his current assets to his son Jamie. I believed we would have time to build our own assets together. Was I in for a surprise!

Now and then. Tom would mention the prenuptial, and I would tell him since he was the one who wanted the prenuptial and he was the one with all the assets, he should have his attorney prepare the document, and I would take it to an attorney to review. I assumed it would be a simple document.

As I began to get busy with wedding preparations and Crystal's high school graduation celebration, Tom spent his time preparing the prenuptial documents. He was a good sport about joining me in helping to chaperone the senior after-graduation all-night party. It turned out to be fun, but we were very tired the next day. That is, we adults, not the kids. Approximately three weeks before the wedding, Tom presented me with the prenuptial draft. This was a thirty-five or so page document and was written in an extremely complicated style. I read the whole document and was genuinely concerned about some of the sections. It seemed unfair. I talked to my friends about the document, and they encouraged me to seek legal counsel. I had no attorney, so I used the yellow pages to find one. Each attorney I called said they would not have enough time to review the document before the wedding and were not interested in taking my case. When I told Tom, he said he would check with his attorney to see if he could recommend anyone. I called each attorney on the list Tom's attorney provided; however, I received the same decline for the same reason. Finally, a semi-retired attorney was referred to me. He was a friend of one of Tom's employees. I contacted this attorney, and he agreed to help, though he reiterated often during our conversation there wasn't time to make changes before the wedding since the date was only a week and a half away. I sent the attorney the draft document and waited for him to respond. In the meantime, I sold or gave away all the furniture I didn't want in my new home. I moved in with Tom about a week before the wedding. When Crystal came back from her senior trip to Mexico, she came to live with us. Crystal would be staying with us until she left for college at the end of the summer. Tom's son, Jamie, was also living with us. He was going to be a senior in high school in the fall. He expressed happiness his family was expanding.

My attorney called me a week before the wedding and said the prenuptial document treated me like a second-class citizen. There were to many areas that needed to be changed, but there wasn't time. I said, "Then let's throw it out and start over with a new one." I was extremely stressed and angry with Tom's attorney. I couldn't understand why he prepared such a one-sided, long, and complicated prenuptial that treated me like a second-class citizen. My attorney said there wasn't time to start over. He said he would prepare a side letter that stated we would make amendments to the prenuptial after the wedding. I discussed my dilemma with my attorney and my friends. I was encouraged to sign the documents and get them amended later. I began to think that once Tom realized that I loved him and did not marry him for his money, he would be happy to amend the document. This is the same thinking I used with my first marriage. It didn't work then, but I thought it would work now since I wasn't dealing with alcoholism.

I signed the side letter that referred to making amendments after the honeymoon, and I signed the prenuptial document the evening before the wedding. Tom presented the documents to me right after the wedding rehearsal dinner. I believe my consumption of wine with dinner, plus the fact we had 250 guests attending the wedding the next day, gave me the incentive to sign.

The wedding was beautiful. The ceremony was held outside on the lawn at the Seattle Tennis Club, and the reception was held inside. The sun was shining, all the guests arrived, and the food was excellent and was displayed with such artistic flair. Marcellus walked me down the aisle, Crystal was my maid of honor, and Marge was my bridesmaid. I was so happy my cousin JR and his family were able to attend. To my delight, they brought Marian and Jack with them. Michael Slover and his wife also were able to attend, and I could see he was so proud of me. His wife said I was one of his successful clients. Michael was the counselor I saw for about a year after I graduated from high school. It was during a time when I was very lost and depressed. I had been living with my sister and her family. Michael was a psychologist. I had sessions with him regularly for over a year. He helped me feel that I actually attend college as I became stronger and stronger. Overall, it was an absolutely beautiful day, and the next morning we were off to Italy on our honeymoon. We arrived in Amsterdam with a half-hour wait for our flight to Italy. Tom called home to see how Jamie and Crystal were doing. Jamie answered and said, "Hi, Dad – I have to go; the police are here." Then he hung up, and when Tom called back, he didn't answer. We had to rush for our gate at that point and almost missed our flight.

We arrived in Napoli, Italy, rented a car, and headed for Positano on the Amalfi Coast. As soon as we checked into our room, Tom called Jamie. Tom relayed to me that Jamie held a party at the house, and it got out of hand when a car loan of uninvited kids tried to get in. The result was a broken window and a very messy house. I called Crystal on her cell phone to get her side of the story. She said Jamie invited a group of his friends over, and when it got late and they wouldn't leave, Crystal packed a bag and went to a friend's house to sleep. When she arrived the next day, she found the house in a mess and Jamie, along with his friends, still sleeping. Crystal cleaned up part of the mess so when Diane, our household manager, showed up on Monday, she wouldn't be faced with a huge mess. Jamie never cleaned up after himself.

We did have fun on our honeymoon during the times I suppressed the frustration Tom caused me through his insensitivity and pushy behavior. I drank wine every evening during our honeymoon so I could relax around Tom. His behavior wouldn't bother me so much during our evenings of dining and sipping wine. There was one very upsetting situation. I have told the story to my friends, and we had lots of laughs over it, but at the time of the incident, I was devastated. We drove to the quaint small town of Ravello on the Amalfi Coast in Italy. We parked near the base of the town and walked up to the entrance since cars were not allowed in the main portion of the town. Tom had previously mentioned to me the town was known for their cameo jewelry. I was so excited to buy a cameo pin or ring. We toured around the town that was incredibly beautiful with fountains, flowers, statues, bougainvillea, and ivy hanging off most buildings. Finally, we walked into the piazza and spotted a jewelry shop. When we entered, I saw a large display of cameo jewelry. I was so delighted. Tom asked me to walk to the back of the store with him. I didn't want to leave the cameo jewelry counter, but I did and followed him throughout the store. I was learning to just go along with Tom to avoid his relentless pushiness. He asked questions about the artifacts on display. Finally, we were in the front of the store, and I was looking at cameos again. Tom pulled me away to look at an exceptionally large aquamarine pendant necklace surrounded with diamonds. I told him it was nice, and I turned away to look at cameos again. Tom asked the storeowner to pull the pendant out of the box. Tom pulled me over again and said he wanted to buy the pendant for me. The price was $6,000. I said, "No, Tom, it's too expensive." He then became very persistent and pushy. I said, "Tom, the piece is too big. When would I ever wear something like that?" He said, "You can wear it to the next Poncho (Patron of the Arts Auction held in Seattle)." I kept insisting that I didn't want the piece. Finally, out of frustration, I walked out of the store. Tom followed me out and kept badgering me. I told him he was making me feel extremely uncomfortable and if I could I have gotten on a plane right there and gone home, I would. He just wouldn't stop. I explained it was too expensive and that I wanted to buy leather goods in Florence and other things while we were on our honeymoon. He said we could still buy those things after we purchased the aquamarine necklace. I just couldn't understand why Tom was determined to buy me something I didn't want. Finally, out of desperation, I said all right. We went back into the store, and he bought the pendant. We left the store and left Ravello with an exceptionally large necklace and no cameo.

After we left the Amalfi coast, we headed for Tuscany. Tom took me on a hot air balloon ride through Tuscany. This was a beautiful experience, but not without its moments of extreme pushiness and frustration. Again, I found myself doing what Tom wanted so he would not become a bully. I found myself thinking about how I did this same thing in my first marriage. Something was not right here, and I knew it, but I kept going along.

Our honeymoon took us to Florence, and as promised, we purchased leather jackets and even a pair of leather pants. I kept telling Tom I thought he was spending too much money, but I soon learned, you could not tell Tom what to do. When you did, he became a bulldog and pushed ahead with what he wanted to do. We were walking across the Ponte Vecchio Bridge, stopping from time to time to look in the small shops that lined both sides of the bridge. Tom spied an 18-karat gold cuff bracelet that he wanted to buy me. Again, I said it was too expensive, but Tom persisted, and I let him buy the $3,000-dollar bracelet for me. When he saw something he wanted to buy, and I tried to talk him out of it, he came up with all kinds of reasons why it was a good buy, and he would be foolish to pass it up. Later that night, he purchased a $7,000 antique altarpiece with a granite top and spent another $3,000 to ship it home. He envisioned using it in a country inn he was planning to build one day. The piece was placed in a vacant space in his industrial park. The country inn was never built.

You may think Tom had the money to purchase these things, so I should have been more receptive and appreciative of his gifts. Tom certainly did have a considerable amount of money; however, I knew he lived off monthly loans from his Development Company and Industrial Park. I also knew he had not set aside funds to cover security deposits he was holding from his tenants for future improvements, or future commissions on new leases. Tom came from a very frugal background, as did I; however, he spent money like there was no end to it.

Months later, when we were dressing for Poncho, Tom went down to the basement to retrieve the aquamarine necklace from his safe. He was gone for quite a while, and I was about to go check on him when he walked into the room. He was breathing hard, his face was red, he was sweating profusely, and he was a little disheveled. When I asked him what was wrong, he explained he couldn't remember the code to the safe, and he was trying to break it open. I asked him if he had the code written down someplace, and I couldn't believe it when he said it was written on a piece of paper and the paper was supposed to be on top of the safe with other papers. I had to work awfully hard to suppress laughter. I found the whole situation to be hysterical and sad at the same time. We determined the household manager threw the papers away when she was cleaning. Tom hid the code under papers on top of the safe because he was afraid he would forget the code and where he had hidden the paper with the code. Needless to say, I did not wear the necklace to Poncho that year. When we returned from the event, I went downstairs to look at the safe. The crowbar Tom had been using was lying on top of the safe, which was all beat up but still closed and locked. He called a locksmith to come the next day to open the safe. He purchased another safe and had it installed in his bedroom closet. He also purchased one for me and it was installed inside my closet. I didn't think I needed one; however, I soon learned Tom would go into his safe and pull out a piece of jewelry for me as a gift for Christmas, my birthday, or any time he wanted to give me a gift. So, basically, he would remove jewelry from his safe and I would place it in my safe. I was certainly very appreciative; however, the jewelry was usually not my style, and I seldom wore it. I would have liked to have Tom pick out a piece of jewelry that I loved, but he would have to think about me and that never happened. His gifts were about Tom. They were given to make him feel good without any regard for my feelings.

When I married Tom, I owned a black Honda Accord, and I really liked my car. One day he came home and showed me pictures of an older model Mercedes and said he wanted to buy it for me. As on so many previous occasions, I protested. I told him I had a car and didn't need another vehicle. His badgering went on for days. Finally, he said Marcellus needed a vehicle, so I should give him my car. I suggested we purchase an inexpensive vehicle for Marcellus. He just needed something to get back and forth to Bellevue Community College. No, Tom did not want to do that. I eventually gave in, and we gave my car to Marcellus, and Tom bought the Mercedes for me. I was very appreciative of the gift of the Mercedes; however, it was not my car of choice, and it was not comfortable. It was an older model 250 SL hard-top and soft-top convertible, but it was too hard for me to remove the hard top by myself, and Tom was never around to help me, so I rarely used it as a convertible.

Our Christmas seasons together became quite a grand and fun celebrations mixed with anxiety and frustration. By this time, I knew that Tom needed to repeat experiences, repeat adventures and repeat conversations; otherwise, he would become completely frazzled and belligerent. So, when Christmas approached, and Tom announced we needed to purchase a large tree to place in the solarium and decorate it for the large party we would be giving with eighty or so guests. I prepared to step in and help plan the party. He gave explicit instructions to Diane, our household manager, as to the exact type and size of tree to have delivered. I dug out all the Christmas decorations from the basement. After Diane had the tree delivered and set up, I found myself, in the very cold month of December in Seattle, out in the cold solarium with only a small radiant heater to keep me warm and only if I were standing in front of it. I was wearing a winter coat and gloves, up on the ladder decorating the Christmas tree. This was not fun. I worked on the tree in the evenings after working all day, and it took me about four days to finish. This activity continued each Christmas season. The second Christmas, Tom came home late one evening, and I told him to come out and help. He only helped for a brief time then stopped and told me to buy tinsel to put on the tree. I said, "Absolutely not." The badgering started again, and I finally said, "Tom, only poor white trash put tinsel on Christmas trees." He said, "Jackie always put tinsel on the tree." I replied, "She did not, Tom." He said he would go upstairs to find the Christmas tapes from past Christmases and prove it to me. He left the solarium, and I was left to work on the tree. When I finally finished, I went upstairs to find Tom in our bedroom still looking through old tapes. He came downstairs later and announced he couldn't find any pictures or tapes with tinsel on the tree. That was the end of the tinsel discussion.

The Christmas parties were always a remarkable success, with delicious food, excellent wine, and good friends and family. Everyone loved the tree, particularly because it had real candles on it for lights. Tom would run around the tree replacing burned-out candles with fresh ones. He loved the attention he received over the lighting of the tree. The next morning was not so great. I got up early to find the dining room and a large living room floor filthy with spilled wine and food crumbs. The large pieces of furniture in our living room furniture had been moved out to the garage to make room. All the rugs were taken up as well. I could have left the mess for Diane to clean up on Monday morning, but that was not like me. I spent all morning washing the wine glasses, silverware, and miscellaneous serving dishes then moved to mopping he floor. Tom would get up around 1:00 p.m. All that was left to do was to move the furniture back into the living room.

Christmas morning had its downside as well. Tom insisted we all go into the solarium to open presents. I'd make hot chocolate, and we'd all be sitting around the Christmas tree sipping hot chocolate while wearing coats over our pajamas. This was no fun for anyone except Tom. He never understood that this was his tradition and not mine or my children's, and that we needed to have a small tree inside the living room where it was warm. It was a battle I chose not to pursue. After the Christmas party, we never re-lit the candles on the tree, not even on Christmas morning. None of us wanted to stay out in the cold solarium any longer than we had to.

As the months went by, I began to see significant changes in Tom. He showed signs of distrusting me; our communication was deteriorating. I had already determined he was narcissistic. I went to see a psychologist to discuss narcissistic personalities. After I explained our situation, she went into detail explaining narcissistic personality disorders. I then understood his personality and behavior would not get better; it would only get worse with age. I realized I had to take care of myself since I couldn't take care of Tom. The meeting notes he left on his desk began to look like mere scribbles and made no sense. Brokers began to ask for me when they called so they wouldn't have to speak to Tom. He began repeating himself and getting off the subject during conversations. I tried to take on more of his work, but this only made him angry with me.

This personality disorder was intensifying, and I believed other mental or physiological changes were occurring. He wouldn't talk with me, he only talked at me, and the topic was generally about him or something he was doing or going to do. If I made a comment during one of his tirades, he would say he had to start all over again. He would start at the beginning, repeating each word deliberately. He could spend hours working on a document, sometimes all night long. The documents often had repeated pages and redundant ideas. I would often clean up his office since he was extremely messy and never put anything away. Whatever landed on his desk stayed on his desk and was never filed. When I first started working for Tom (about 10 years earlier) I was told not to touch anything on his desk. You couldn't see the top of his desk because papers were about half an inch thick and completely covered the entire desk. Once when Tom took his family on vacation, I decided to clean off his desk. This took me all day. When he returned from vacation, he walked into his office and immediately walked back to my desk and asked what I had done with all his papers. He looked very distraught and upset. I replied, "I threw them in the trash since I figured they weren't important anymore." He had such a shocked look on his face, I immediately told him I was just kidding. I filed what I could, and the remainder was in his in-basket. From that time on, he let me clean off his desk.

One night we were coming home from dinner after being out with our friends Bill and Darlene. We were taking them to our home where their car was parked. Bill and Darlene were in the back seat, Tom was driving, and I was sitting next to Tom. We came up to an intersection, and the light was red. Tom did not slow down but sped through the intersection. I was shocked. I asked Tom if he'd seen the red light, and he said he hadn't. I knew Bill and Darlene had to be terribly nervous if not terrified. When I tried to talk to him about what he had done, he became agitated and suggested since he didn't cause an accident, I should stop talking about it. Bill and Darlene did not say a word. I kept thinking the car could have been hit by another vehicle in the back area of the car and Darlene and Bill could have been injured.

Another bad driving experience was when just the two of us coming home from an evening out. Tom stopped at a red stoplight, and when it turned green, we just sat there. I looked over at him; he was sound asleep. Another time we had just left a fundraising event that was celebrating Habitat for Humanity. This is an organization that helps people obtain a home. On the way home, I mentioned I would never know what it felt like to own a home since I was just a guest in Tom's home. He said, "Oh honey, you'd have to move if anything happened to me because you couldn't afford the taxes." When I asked why he wouldn't want to leave me with means to support myself, he only replied he would have to abide by the prenuptial document. I knew then I was not only a guest in his house; I was also a guest in the marriage and in his business. I felt used, incredibly sad and lonely. I would find myself thinking, "What have I gotten myself into?"

There were occasions when Tom would behave like a five-year-old. Once when we were getting ready for work and were having a disagreement, Tom walked into the bedroom where I was getting dressed and screamed at me. I told him to stop, and he flung himself to the floor on his hands and knees and began pounding his feet and fists on the floor, crying and wailing like a small child. I just stood there watching him, frozen, unable to speak. I then quickly left the room and went downstairs, where I tried to catch my breath and compose myself. This was bizarre behavior for a fifty-six-year-old man. When I heard him come down and enter his office, I went back up to the bedroom to finish putting on my makeup and combing my hair. Tom soon came back into the bedroom spouting. "Honey, I finally figured what's the matter." "What?" I asked. "You think I'm crazy," he said. I took a deep breath and quietly and calmly said, "No, Tom, I don't think you are crazy, because if you were crazy, that behavior would be forgivable. Since you are not crazy, that behavior is very inappropriate, and you had better never do that again." He turned around and walked out of the room.

I eventually told him I was worried about him and our relationship. I suggested a therapist for both of us. To my surprise, he agreed. We visited a therapist together for about a year, and I could see no improvement. His distrust of me increased, and he began to shut me out of the business. Communication was almost non-existent. Our disagreements increased. He could never admit partial fault or responsibility. His behavior toward me was that of a pest. He would yell, stomp around and leave the room. Upon his return, he acted like nothing happened or that I was making up problems. I began to feel extreme anxiety and began to lose sleep and weight. I also went with him to see his medical doctor. He put Tom on Adderall medication for attention deficit disorder, which caused him to spend longer amounts of time on the computer. He rarely went to bed before 4:00 a.m. and was up by 7:30 a.m. I tried to get him to understand he should not be taking Adderall because it was having the opposite effect of what it was supposed to do. I was at such a loss about what to do, and it seemed no one really understood what was going on. His arguments with Jamie increased, and Jamie would usually quickly leave the house shouting that his dad was crazy. I was beginning to think about what the private therapist I saw once who said to me, "You need to take care of myself," but at this time, I didn't know what to do.

I put my worries aside in the spring of 2004 and began to concentrate on Crystal's graduation from college. I was filled with pride at all her accomplishments. She graduated in four years, became a resident of California to qualify for in-state tuition after the first semester of her freshman year, thus reducing tuition costs. In the summer after her freshman year, she traded in her little sporty car for a Nissan Pathfinder and drove herself back to San Diego for her sophomore year. Marcellus and I flew down to San Diego to help her move from the dorm into an apartment with girlfriends. We bought furniture from Ikea for her apartment, and Marcellus helped set it all up. The next three years flew by. I was so proud of her as I saw her maturing into a lovely young lady. I now wanted her graduation and her gift from me to be special. I was filled with pride as I watched her walk down the aisle to receive her diploma. After graduation, we held a dinner for her at an Italian restaurant in La Jolla, California. Her father was able to attend and gave her a beautiful watch. I was pleased. Later that evening, I thanked Marcellus for telling his father that under no circumstances was he to show up for his sister's graduation without a very meaningful gift because that would break her heart again. He said he told his dad he had four years to save money for a gift, and he better come through this time. Tom and I gave her an aquamarine ring earlier that day. I handmade a graduation card for her showing pictures of Italy on the front. When she opened it up, she saw something like, "You are in receipt of a trip to Italy. — Mother." I gave her the card during dinner. She was excited about the whole evening, and I know it was a very memorable graduation for her.

Within a week after she arrived home from college with her Pathfinder loaded to the top, we began packing for Italy. I used all of

Tom's frequent flyer miles for the airfare, so there was no cost to us. Even though we had money, I was trying to be as frugal as I could. The week was a wonderful experience for the two of us. I kept a journal of each day of our trip and after we arrived home, I set out to make a book filled with travel memories, pictures, receipts and thoughts. Also, I bought a cameo ring when we were in Rome. I hesitated in spending the $400 for the cameo ring. We left the store without the ring and headed to the nearest outdoor bar. After finishing my glass of wine, I said, "Let's go back to the shop and buy the ring."

It was the summer of 2004; Crystal and I had been back from our trip to Italy. It was a warm summer afternoon, and I was sunning in the back yard while reading a book, Tom was in his office, and Crystal was upstairs in her room. Earlier that morning, I presented Tom with a printout of our expenses the last four years since he had been claiming I had spent all his money. He came out and sat down and proceeded to drill me about what happened to all his money. I kept requesting he refer to the spreadsheet that was a detailed cash flow of income and expenses over the last four years. He kept saying, "I don't understand; what happened to all my money?" I kept saying, "You spent it, Tom." He would bellow for a few minutes then go back into the house. Soon he would be back bellowing and claiming he didn't understand. This went on and on for a major part of the afternoon. Finally, I said, "Tom, just admit you spent the money and let me help you going forward to curb your spending." He was almost crying, bellowing and stammering. He finally went back into the house. I decided I'd had enough of his bizarre behavior, so I went upstairs to change clothes. Crystal asked me if I wanted to go to a movie with her, and I gladly agreed. When we were in the car, Crystal said, "Mom, I could hear everything from my bedroom window, and I just don't understand why you didn't get angry or raise your voice at Tom." I explained to her it wasn't really about me; it was all about Tom. Her next question was, "Mom, what would you do if you heard my boyfriend talk to me the way Tom talked to you?" I paused for a moment, then responded, "I'd shoot the son of a bitch." "Now you know how I feel about Tom" was her reply.

Our situation at work grew worse. When tenants of the industrial park wanted to renew their lease, they would ask me if I could work out the details with them so they wouldn't have to talk to Tom. Tom's communication skills deteriorated and became very erratic. Tom showed jealously and frustration instead of complimenting me on my lease negotiation skills. This led to constant friction at work. He also ordered his accounting firm to not have any contact with me. I had always been the one to communicate directly with them in all the past years and now they wouldn't speak to me or return my calls. I didn't understand what was going on until the assistant accountant did take my call and said that Tom had ordered the firm to not talk to me or give me any information. At that time brokers would call and only want to talk with me. Tom would turn a simple transaction into a long-drawn-out ordeal. He was not capable of closing a deal.

Our neighbor at the industrial park expressed interest in purchasing the vacant lot between our two properties so they could expand their water bottling business. Tom owned this lot and had been holding on to it with the idea of selling it someday. Also, during this time, the vacancy at the industrial park, owned by Tom, was so high it was a struggle to meet mortgage payments and keep up with the draws he took each month. I was so relieved to learn about the possibility of selling the property. I knew the property was worth at least $1 million, and this would be enough to pay down credit lines and put away enough to cover us for pending tenant improvements so that we could obtain new leases for the vacant spaces. Tom started out negotiating with our neighbor, but eventually, I joined in the meetings to help keep the talking going. I had received a call from the neighbor expressing frustration with Tom, so I talked Tom into letting me sit in. This lasted about three weeks until Tom announced he did not want me involved because he felt I was taking our neighbor's side in the negotiations. Tom was asking $2 million for the property and our neighbor was willing to pay $1.2 million. I knew the offer was very fair but could not convince Tom.

Tom had earlier promised I could buy the car I wanted as soon as the lot sale came to fruition. We were watching a commercial one night, and the driver of the car expressed how he loved his car. Tom said that's how he felt about his Alfa Romeo. I said I didn't feel that way about my Mercedes, and that's when he said I should have the car I really wanted as soon as the sale of the lot went through. This gave me even more incentive to help with the negotiations. I received another call from our neighbor, stating he was so tired of arguing with Tom and did not want to proceed with the purchase and sale agreement discussions. I explained to our neighbor that we really needed the cash from the sale. I told him he had to figure out a way to show how Tom would be the one gaining from this deal. Eventually, he came up a proposition that worked. He added a clause in the purchase and sale agreement that stated his company would lease out almost 20,000 square feet of warehouse for a year while construction was taking place for their expanded building. Tom finally saw this as a win-win for him, and he was able to agree to the purchase price of $1.2 million. After the funds were in the industrial park bank, I reminded Tom, he had promised me I could purchase a new car. I found a buyer for the Mercedes, and Tom expressed his willingness to have me purchase a new car. He wanted me to buy a new Mercedes; however, I settled on a new BMW. When the vehicle arrived at the dealership, Tom wanted to go with me to purchase the car. I was smarter now. I knew if Tom went with me, he would put the car in his name, and I would be without a vehicle altogether. That's what he did with the Mercedes. I told Tom the vehicle had a complicated computer, and I needed to take Crystal with me because she could understand how the computer worked better than me. I told him I needed her there when the computer was explained to me. He agreed that was a great idea and wrote out a check to pay for the vehicle in full and handed the check to me. I was so relieved that my car would be in my name.

Tom soon hired an individual named Stan to help him develop vacant land that Tom owned. Stan was a general contractor who had been performing tenant improvement construction jobs at the industrial park for the past eight years. Stan became Tom's right-hand man, and eventually Tom told me not to have any contact with the tenants because Stan would be doing that from now on. I was stripped of all my responsibilities.

It was toward the end of August of 2004, and I suggested Tom take a vacation with Jamie. I thought the time away would help him relax, and I hoped things would be better after they returned. He liked the idea but didn't know where to go. Since Jamie had shown an interest in boats, I suggested taking a trip to Southern California. He spent a good part of a Saturday afternoon planning the trip. I was so surprised when he finally announced they were going to Italy to watch the formula one car races. They planned to be gone for two weeks, and I was looking forward to peace and quiet while Tom was away.

During the first week he was gone, he would call and yell at me if I informed him of my discussions with tenants. He told me to stop talking to his tenants. He said he wanted Stan to completely take over my job. Days later, he called to say his wallet was stolen. This was no surprise to me. Tom insisted on carrying his breast coat wallet in his jeans back pocket. This meant half of it was sticking out. His wallet was always crammed full of credit cards, spare checks to more than one checking account and small pieces of paper. I transferred the funds from our joint account into my personal account so no one could tap into those accounts. I called our household manager, Diane, and told her what happened, and she proceeded to contact the bank and all credit card companies. She wired Tom funds and new credit cards so he and Jamie could continue their trip.

He called and yelled at me one more time while he was on his trip, and this was only Thursday of the first week. I was really hurt and angry. Shortly after I hung up the phone, Stan walked into my office to tell me about a meeting he had with one of our tenants. I was still hurt and angry and just looked up and said, "It doesn't matter, Stan, because I'm out of here." When he asked what that meant, I replied, "First I'm leaving Broadmoor, then I'm leaving Preston." Our company and industrial park were in Preston, and our home was in the Broadmoor community of Seattle. He just looked at me and walked away.

The following Friday evening Crystal asked what plans I had for the weekend. I told her I would be packing. She looked at me with a surprised look on her face. "What do you mean, Mom?" she asked. When I told her I had reached my limit and was moving out, she became so excited and she said, "Well, I'm packing too, and I'm so happy I finally got my mom back!"

We packed all weekend and each night during the week right after work, saying not a word to anyone. Our household manager, Diane, was on vacation that week and didn't know what I was doing. I didn't want Tom to be upset with her, so I kept her in the dark. Marcellus rented a truck, and we hauled all our belongings to storage. Crystal and I planned to stay with my adopted parents, Mavis and Angus, for a brief period of time. I adopted them years earlier since both my parents were no longer living. I was talking to Mavis one day, and I mentioned that we don't get a chance to choose our parents, but if we did, I would choose her. She immediately said I should adopt her. Just then Angus walked into the room and Mavis told him about our conversation. He looked at us and said, "Well, then that means I'm her adopted father, right?' I said, "of course," and from that time on, they were my adopted parents. That Saturday night, after I was all settled in at their home, I called Diane to tell her what I had done. I wanted to prepare her for what she might walk into on Monday morning. Tom was scheduled to arrive that Sunday evening. She was a little surprised but understood the whole situation. She had observed situations during the past four years. She was so glad I moved out without telling her beforehand so Tom would not be angry with her for not informing him.

Tom called me that evening and was terribly upset. He didn't seem to be upset that I moved out, only that, in his words, "You stole some of my possessions and I want them back." I explained that I only took what he had bought for me, but in his mind, since he used his money, everything was his, and he had a prenuptial to prove he owned everything. After a long unsuccessful telephone conversation, we made a date to meet at a local restaurant the next morning. I arrived on time and began to wait for Tom. After about a half-hour of waiting, I ordered breakfast, ate my breakfast, and paid for my breakfast. Finally, Tom showed up, an hour late. Our discussion didn't go well. All Tom could focus on was that I had abandoned him and that I stole his personal belongings. He said I needed to give back what I stole. Finally, out of desperate frustration, I said goodbye and left the restaurant.

I received a call late in the afternoon from my friend Darlene. Tom had called them, and they invited him to come over so they could talk to him. I had already informed them the week I was packing to move out. They were not surprised. They had seen a change in Tom in the past couple of years. She told me Tom was at their house and had been there all afternoon. She and her husband, Bill, were trying to help Tom understand our situation from my point of view, but he just wasn't capable. He was adamant about me coming back home and bringing all the things I stole. Darlene sounded very tired and disappointed at not being able to help. She then said half joking that I should go back to the house and get more of Tom's furnishings. I thanked them for their help but was not surprised at the outcome. I knew I was not going back.

Crystal and I began looking for an apartment for the two of us. I didn't know how long Tom would let me continue to work in his company, and Crystal hadn't had time to even look for a job. We found an apartment in Redmond and called upon Marcellus to help us move. He became our go-to guy for help in moving. He would call up his guy friends and they would always show up ready to help, knowing their pay would only be pizza and beer. They weren't professional movers, but the price was right during the times we didn't have extra money to go toward moving expenses.

I Always Felt Safe with Rick

Rick Acton, The Love of My Life
And My Best Friend

Wedding Day 7/8/2000

Gloria & Giorgio Filocamo at the
Cameo Shop [he's happy]

The Aquamarine, 173 ct.
Diamonds 1.26 ct.
[I wore once]

Tom Loved Christmas

"The Christmas Tree" in the Solarium
[very, very cold]

July 8, 2000 - Wedding
Marcellus, Crystal, Me, Tom and Jamie

The Cameo Shop in Ravello, Italy

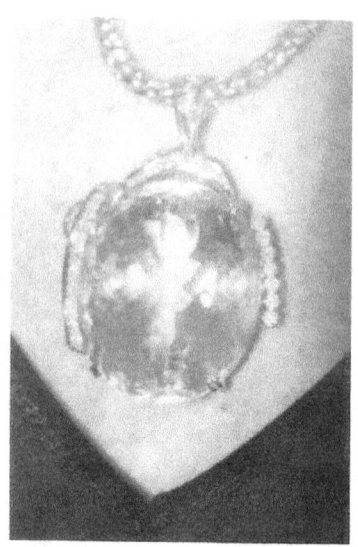

The Aquamarine, 173 ct.

Diamonds 1.26 ct.

[I wore it once]

My substitute Necklace and

Tom Looking Very Stressed

Happier Times

My substitute Necklace and
Tom Looking Very Stressed

Solarium in summer (warm)

Pondering My Future or frustrated

My Sister at age 45

My Sister in 2015

The Mercedes I pretended to like.

# VIII
## "A Six Year Divorce"

I knew the divorce would be difficult; I had no idea just how difficult. I made an appointment to see a psychologist who specializes in narcissistic behavior. After explaining my circumstances to her during my first and only meeting, she gave me the name of an attorney and suggested I call the attorney right away and get ready for an exceedingly long and expensive divorce. I made the call and scheduled an appointment.

The divorce took six years. The first year Crystal and I were living together in an apartment, and we were both unemployed. My attorney was able to get Tom to agree to continue paying my salary even though I was no longer working for his company. It took me about a year until I found employment. During that year I would spend part of the day looking for work and the other part working on preparation for the divorce court. Crystal obtained employment after about nine months and moved out on her own. Though I was tangled up in the divorce, I moved on with my life. We went to trial at the Superior Court in Seattle. Tom's attorney was claiming the prenuptial was valid, and I deserved nothing. My attorney was claiming the prenuptial was invalid; therefore, I was entitled to half of the community property. There was a plethora of questions to answer, both written and verbal, during the deposition period. There were thick documents to review and sign and research to complete. Tom and his attorney were trying to make him look like a hero, with all his gifts and the support he gave to my children and me, while trying to make me look like an ungrateful gold digger. All this so-called fact-finding took approximately two years. When the trial started, I felt like the judge was against me. Tom's attorney was really trying to make me look bad. One afternoon he was grilling me with questions about when I was raising my two children. Such questions as, did I set aside money for their college education, did I set up insurance plans for them, so on and so forth. I looked over at my two attorneys for a sign of what to do, but they just looked at me with frustration on their faces. I then said to Tom's attorney, "You have no idea what it's like to raise two children all by yourself; otherwise, you wouldn't be asking me such silly questions." He immediately said he had no more questions and sat down. My attorney's approach was to merely show that the whole prenuptial, before, during and after, was extremely one-sided. Tom admitted that he wrote the prenuptial. His attorney gave him a boilerplate document, and Tom prepared the entire prenuptial. Now I understood why it was written in such a one-sided manner and why it was so long. All this time, I thought his attorney had written the document. The prenuptial stated I had to put half of my monthly salary into the community property checking account, but the money Tom drew from his company was not community property. Tom would draw out anywhere from $800 thousand to $1 million each year that was not considered community property money, and I had to put in $30,000 (half the salary I earned) into the community property account. Therefore, I was the only one contributing to community property. So, according to the documents, there was no community property. Tom's attorney tried to show that I was highly intelligent, was used to reading overly complicated purchase and sale agreements as well as commercial leases, and therefore, knew what I was signing. I remember sitting very still thinking, *well, I paid for Crystal's education, not Tom. I put half of my money into the community property account and also helped Crystal with money from my own personal account. Tom looks like a very generous individual. Actually, he is but only if it benefits him.*

My two attorneys suggested I have a full psychological evaluation done to show that it was not in my nature or mental capacity to be dishonest. This led to days of test-taking by a psychiatrist in Seattle, plus a couple of counseling sessions. There was something about the psychiatrist that I didn't like, but I wasn't sure exactly what. He prepared a lengthy document that stated I was an intelligent, very honest and loyal person and that when under stress, I would freeze and regress to the emotional state of a child. I was in that state when I signed the document, and I just hoped things would turn out for the best. Years later I learned this psychiatrist committed suicide when it was discovered he had a camera in the women's bathroom so he could watch any time a woman entered the bathroom. I knew there was something about him that I didn't like, but I would have never guessed he was a voyeur or pervert.

The trial lasted three days, and the day the judge was to give her decision, I was extremely nervous. I wasn't sure the judge saw through all the rhetoric and nonsense Tom's attorney threw out to make me look bad and Tom look so great. To my relief, the Judge ruled the prenuptial was invalid and unenforceable. She said the document itself was unfair, and the situation leading up to the signing of the document was unfair. She said it was written so that there would never be community property, and he controlled my salary. It was unfair that I had to give half my salary to the joint account each month. She said Tom waited too long before he gave me the document, which kept me from getting proper representation. The Judge stated she knew her decision would be appealed, so she was careful throughout the trial making sure no one could find fault in the proceedings.

Tom appealed her decision. Much to my disappointment, we had to prepare for the Appellate Court, and Tom and I were still married. I had to obtain another lawyer who had experience in the Appellate Court. Thus far Tom was paying my attorney fees because he was the one forcing the lawsuit and he was the one with the funds to pay the attorney fees. I was feeling the anxiety creep in again. The soonest we could get an Appellate Court date was two years into the future. My new attorney spent time reviewing all the court documents and prepared her presentation to the court. Documents from both sides were sent to the court, and on the actual court date, both attorneys made their pleadings to the four appellate court judges, and we waited about a week for their response. The news came in the form of an email from my attorneys; the appellate court ruled in my favor. The prenuptial was unenforceable and invalid. I was so relieved until my attorney told me Tom was appealing. The anxiety came back. Yes, Tom appealed the Appeals Court ruling. We were still married.

It was about this time that Crystal was planning to enter a Bikram Yoga school and needed financial help. She obtained a second job to help save for the money, but she still needed help. I called Tom and asked him if he would like to buy back the aquamarine necklace he bought me on our honeymoon and a silver fox fur coat that he had given me. I told him I'd sell them to him for $4,000, and I waited for his answer. This is the same necklace he bought for $6,000 and the coat once belonged to Jackie, his first wife. It was too large for me, and I only wore it a couple of times. I don't believe Jackie wore it much because she was smaller than me. It didn't take him long to respond that he would buy the necklace and coat. I told him I didn't mean to insult him, but I needed him to pay me with a cashier's check. I only wore the necklace once. It was just too big for me. A local jewelry store was not able to sell it after having it in the store window for a year. The owner said women loved it and tried it on but would say they had no place to wear it. The necklace was just a status symbol for Tom. The next day I met Diane in the parking lot of a local restaurant, and we exchanged the necklace and coat for the cashier's check. She said Tom wasn't quite sure which necklace I was talking about, but that didn't stop him from wanting it back. He wanted all the jewelry back that he had given me. I gave the $4,000 to Crystal to pay the balance due on the yoga school tuition.

Yes, Tom appealed to State Supreme Court, and we were still married. A year and a half went by, and we were scheduled to appear at the State Supreme Court in Olympia. Again, my attorney had to send documents to the State Supreme Court and prepare her pleading to present to the seven judges. Crystal drove me down to Olympia on the date of the hearing. We met my attorney and sat down to wait for the judges to enter the large courtroom that was mostly empty except for Tom and his attorney and about eight people waiting to plead their case. The judges appeared shocked when they learned Tom and I were still married after six years from the time we first filed. Normally, a divorce would have been finalized at the first trial; however, Tom wanted to wait because he just felt he would eventually win, and I would end up with nothing.

At this point, I really had no idea if the court would rule in my favor again. I did know that this was the highest court. Tom could take the case no further. However, they ruled, it would be the final decision. My attorney felt good because nothing had happened in the first court that could be looked on as an error or mistake. A week or so went by, and I was feeling anxious about the ruling. I just wanted to win and receive enough money to pay off the balance owed to my attorneys and put a down payment on a house. I was still renting, still feeling insecure and still suffering from anxiety.

Finally, I received a call from my appeals attorney and an email from my other two attorneys. The Supreme Court ruled in my favor! It was finally over. Well, almost. We can throw the prenuptial away and focus on a settlement amount and get the divorce over with. I found out later that our case was used as an example to educate attorneys on how not to write a prenuptial. It's public record for everyone to read.

During these five and a half years, Tom's condition had deteriorated considerably. He no longer worked, and Stan was in charge of negotiating with me. At this time, I learned Jamie had called a close friend of Tom's to come and check things out because Jamie had an idea there was dishonesty going on with Stan and he called Bill to come and look over the company. Bill came on board to run the company and to clean up all the messes Stan and Tom's attorneys had made involving estates, properties, trusts, and debts. Stan and Tom's attorneys were draining the company. After more negotiating with Stan, a settlement amount was agreed upon. However, Tom would not sign. Finally, Tom's attorney appointed a guardian to sign for him. His guardian also signed the divorce decree documents. When Bill stepped in to oversee Tom's assets and to run his company, he cut Tom's attorneys and Stan off from receiving any funds until I was paid in full. At this time, Tom was in an assisted living home. He could no longer walk or talk and needed constant care. I believe he may have forgotten he had a son, as his memory was failing rapidly. Months later, Jamie visited his father at the nursing home. He was so distraught after the visit, he shot himself and died. Knowing Jamie as I did, I know it was an accident done in a state of rage. Jamie would often display anger and go into a violent rage. He would scream, shout, throw things, hit walls, and then abruptly leave the room or house, get into his car, and drive away. Shortly after Jamie's funeral, Tom died from complications stemming from dementia.

I attended both Tom and Jamie's funerals and spoke to the guests about each of them. I was incredibly sad for them and for the whole family. It's hard to believe a whole family could be gone in such a brief period of time.

I took a portion of the money I received from our divorce, paid off the balance of $75,000 owed to my attorneys, purchased a townhome, got busy furnishing my new place and began enjoying my new feeling of security and calmness. Once again, the anxiety began to subside.

# IV
## "Sis"

One afternoon as I got into my car after working out at the local gym, I noticed I had missed a call on my cell phone. I didn't recognize the number, but I saw there was a message. I began listening to the message. The message started out, "Hi, this is your sister." I was wondering who left this message and thinking how mean it was since my sister disowned me over twenty-five years ago. The message went on to say she hoped I didn't mind her calling, but she wanted to get in touch with me, so she got my telephone number from our cousin Jimmy. When she said, "Jimmy," I knew it was my sister. She and I were the only ones who still called our cousin Jimmy. Jimmy was his name when we were young, but when he became an adult, everyone called him JR. That is, everyone except my sister and me.

As I drove home, I began to reflect on the past. My sister and I were close when we were young. She always took care of me and protected me. When we were growing up, she went by her real name, Florence. When she was about to start high school, she started going by a nickname given to her by a friend. Franki became her new name. After I graduated from high school and lived with her and her husband, I noticed she could become bossy and often took on the role of mother. This sometimes led to fights, but we were still close. When I was in college, I would visit her and my two nephews, and that's when I noticed a change in her. She was suffering from constant migraines and depression, so I would stay the weekend to help with the housework and to make sure my nephews had fun. I noticed at times she would talk in a slightly different voice, and I would ask what was wrong or why was she talking differently. She said nothing was wrong and her voice was what it was. Sometimes when we would go out to the nightclubs to meet her friends, she would get angry with me, and I would often leave by myself to get away from her wrath. There were times when she would drive down to Eugene to visit me, she would stay for only an hour or so and then decide to drive back home. I assumed she was just depressed. During this time, she tried to commit suicide twice that I know of. I made a promise to myself that I would take care of her two boys, Tony and Eric, if anything ever happened to her. I hoped she would get better since she was still seeing a counselor.

I remember when I was five months pregnant with Marcellus, she called to say she was getting married and asked me to be in her wedding. I was so happy and excited for her. The following week she called to say she had just realized I would be seven months pregnant on the day of her wedding, and she was afraid I would take the attention away from her, so she decided she did not want me to attend her wedding. It was a confusing and hurtful phone conversation, and she sounded so strange. After we ended our conversation, I cried. I was so hurt, upset, and completely confused. I couldn't understand why she could be so cruel to me.

Years went by without us speaking except an occasional short phone call. I was now living in the Seattle, Washington, area, and she was living in Salem, Oregon. When I told her I was pregnant and the baby was a girl, she was excited. She called me a week after I was home from delivering Crystal and said she wanted to come for a long weekend to help me take care of Crystal. I was so excited and happy since it had been years since I last saw her. I thought perhaps we could be close again because I missed having a sister. Much to my surprise, she showed up on a Friday afternoon with a new boyfriend. We didn't have time to talk because she was entertaining her boyfriend as well. They would leave after breakfast to go tour Seattle and would return in time for dinner. Once she told me I should rest more, but she never offered to help. When they left on Sunday afternoon, I was relieved. I was once again very confused. She looked like my sister, but her behavior was quite different from what I remembered. I thought to myself, *"I don't know who that was, but I'm sure glad she's gone."* Her visit was stressful for me.

During this period, our mother was living across Puget Sound at a Veterans Home in Retzil, Washington. From time to time, I would either bring my mom over to my home for a visit or the children and I would catch the ferry and take a trip to visit her on a Saturday. She would tell me that my sister paid her a visit, but she always asked our mom not to tell me. She told Mom she didn't want to see me and didn't want me to know she was in the area. Mom and I never understood what that was all about. That must have been the beginning of her deciding she didn't want me in her life.

Months later, she called to tell me she was leaving for California with a new boyfriend. She gave her house to the bank, quit her job, and was heading out. She said she would let me know how to reach her after she got settled. After her move to California, we would go for years without speaking to each other. There were times, my nephews would call me to tell me how she was since she didn't have a phone. She told them to not have anything to do with me, but they knew I loved her and would want to know she was all right. I hadn't seen her since Crystal was born.

It was about a year after the kids and I were living in our apartment, my sister called to invite me to visit her in California. She said she was living in Santa Cruz and couldn't wait to see me. I made my plans to fly down and was looking forward to our weekend visit. I came home from work one day and found a message on my phone from my sister. Her message said, "Dad came to me in a dream and said to beware of you." In her dream, he told her to not involve me in her life. She ended the message by saying, "I can't ever see you again." Well, here was another moment of tears, hurt feelings, and confusion. I canceled my trip.

I hadn't heard from her in twenty-five years until I heard the message on my cell phone. When I reached home, I called JR. He said he hoped I wasn't mad he gave her my telephone number. He said she sounded good on the phone. After talking to him, I felt brave enough to give her a call. I was a bit nervous, as I had no idea what to expect. We talked for quite a while, and I said I'd call her again on Saturday morning. Those phone calls lasted two years, with us talking every Saturday morning. I would call her at 9:00 a.m. every Saturday so the call wouldn't be a cost her. I visited her twice when she traveled to Salem, Oregon, to spend two weeks during Christmas and again in the summer visiting her two boys and their family. She is a grandmother of eight.

The first time we met after so many years, I knew I needed added support. I was nervous. I kept remembering how mean and cold she had been to me in the past. I drove to Oregon on a Friday night and stayed with our cousin JR and his wife, Diane. The plan was to meet her at the home of her son, Tony, and then take her to lunch at a restaurant called Annette's. I invited my friend Marge to meet us at the restaurant. Rather, I begged her to come because I needed her there for support. She was more like a sister to me than my own sister. Both Marge and Sharlene were like family to me.

We arrived at Tony's home around eleven. I remember being so nervous. I watched her as she walked out of the front door toward the car. She looked older than I thought she would, and she walked very gingerly. She also had a large smile on her face. I got out and walked up to her, and we both gave each other a long hug. We both had tears in our eyes. We visited for a while at Tony's then left for the restaurant.

I ordered a mimosa, and since she had never had one, she decided to order one. She liked the drink so much she ordered another one. During our breakfast, she told me she had had multiple personalities for years but let them all go during her last therapy treatment. She explained that she was hospitalized twice for mental issues after she moved to California. She did not remember disowning me nor did she remember making the call that canceled our planned visit over twenty-five years ago that ended our relationship. She said she was bi-polar, suffered from chronic migraines and multiple sclerosis. She also explained that in one of her therapy sessions, the therapist looked at her as he leaned forward and asked, "how many people do you have in there?" That's when she realized she had multiple personalities that had been causing her havoc for years. She was pleased to report she only had one now. Not everyone at the table heard this story, so I asked my sister if I could tell them. She said, "Sure." After I told them, we discussed multiple personalities for a while. It was so natural to discuss her situation. There was no embarrassment from anyone.

Well, that explained things. I had seen the personalities in the past but didn't understand them, nor did I know what was going on. I saw two of them. One when we were in college and she would get so angry with me over nothing, and the one she brought with her when she visited when Crystal was an infant. I understood why she didn't remember the things she did or said. She didn't remember visiting our mother in the Veterans Home near where I live, nor did she remember telling Mother to not tell me when she was coming for a visit. She also didn't remember she told Mom she didn't want to see me. We had a good laugh when I said I was glad she settled on her current personality because now she is so sweet, gentle and caring.

She was back to using Florence again, but I just called her Sis. She was very frail for being only a year and a half older than me. I planned a trip to Santa Cruz to visit her, sometime the next summer. It was too difficult and expensive for her to travel. She was in a good place now. She was on public assistance, had a nice apartment, many friends, including a boyfriend, and seemed to be at peace and happy.

I finally had my sister back, but now I was stronger. It was my turn to take care of my sis as she took care of me when we were little girls. I had grown since that frightening day I looked out the back window of the car to watch the fire as it burned all our possessions while at the same time being worried I might turn into a pillar of stone. I was looking forward to years of enjoying my sister.

I eventually made the trip to Santa Cruz, and now I can say, "I will not make that trip again and that was the last time I will see her." This time it is my decision. I flew to San Jose, rented a car, and headed through the very narrow and winding road to the coast. My sister received me with a big welcoming hug. She seemed quite happy to have me there and took immense pleasure in introducing me to her friends. The hotel where she lived was not fancy, but it was clean and quaint. Since she was on disability, the State paid her rent. There were rooms you could rent by the night and rooms to rent by the month or longer. Her apartment included a full kitchen (though small), living room and bedroom. There was a coffee shop next door to the hotel, and that's where my sister met her friends almost every morning for coffee.

We enjoyed catching up and getting reunited that afternoon and for the two days that followed. We walked along the waterfront pier, spent time in the local restaurants, and shared dinners together. To my surprise, our days and evenings revolved around her "timeouts," as she would say, "smoke a bowl" of marijuana. This is the term she used. This started first thing in the morning and continued throughout the day and into the night. We did not venture too far from her apartment so that she could easily go in to smoke a bowl. When 5 o'clock arrived each afternoon, it was time to party, so she would open a large can of beer and fill up her pipe. She consumed only one can of beer a day and would often take hours to finish the beer. She would pick up her guitar and strum a little and sing a song she wrote in between sips of beer. I also saw her drifting from one thought to another, depending on how much pot she had consumed. In the evenings, she would have her one can of beer, and I would have my glass or two of wine.

I met four of her male friends and one female friend. They were a mixture of individuals, each displaying a type of mental weakness, and they all smoked pot every day and every evening. There were Vietnam veterans, and most were on disability. They were all nice to her and to me and seemed to be in good spirits. They kept tabs on each other, and if someone did not show up for coffee, they would go and check on them.

During this weekend, I learned she had suffered at least two nervous breakdowns while living in Santa Cruz. She said the last one was when she was living at the hotel, which was good because her friends got help for her. I was pleased to find this out since I now knew she had a safe place to live. I asked her what happened when she had this breakdown. She said she had stopped taking her medication for her bi-polar disorder, and they told her she began walking around the hotel naked. When medical aides came to get her, she opened the door naked, and they suggested she put on clothes on before they ushered her out the front door of the hotel. She said she was laughing hysterically. She said while she was in the hospital, during one of her counseling sessions, her therapist asked her, "How many of you are in there?" After more therapy, she was able to let go of two personalities and now only had one. I wasn't totally convinced of that. I could see there was another personality hiding inside just waiting for the right time to emerge.

By Sunday, I realized her personality was changing a little. I asked her a couple of questions about her boyfriend, and she became very irritated. She finally responded in an angry tone, "You seem very interested in my boyfriend!" I tried to explain I just wanted to make sure he was good to her and for her. To me, he looked like an "old stoner." She had previously mentioned that he was always broke and she often fed him or gave him money. On my last morning she announced her boyfriend was coming over, I was getting ready to boil an egg for breakfast, so I asked, "Should I put one or two in for him?" She looked at me from across the room and responded in an angry voice, "He's my boyfriend, not yours. If anyone is going to fix him an egg, it will be me." When her boyfriend arrived, I noticed her personality change. I saw the little girl I hadn't seen in years. Her voice changed to that of a child with a hint of soft whining. She sat next to him on the sofa and seemed to forget I was in the room. He and I talked back and forth, but my sister did not say a word. When she finally spoke, her comments were directed to her boyfriend with playful interjected laughter.

His visit was short, and I quickly packed and was ready to leave. I waved to her standing on the street. We agreed I would call her on the next Saturday at 9:00 a.m. as we had done for the last two years. If I were ever late in calling her, she would call me and was always concerned that something might be wrong. This particular morning, it was about five minutes before 9:00 a.m. My phone rang. It was my sister. She said she didn't want to wait around for my call every Saturday and furthermore, she did not want to talk to me again. My short response was, "Okay." She immediately hung up, and we haven't spoken to each other since.

My Sister at age 45

My Sister in 2015

The Mercedes I pretended to like.

# X
## Reflections

So many years have passed. I am now seventy-two years old. As I look back over my life, I find a common thread of constant struggle to move from a place of anxiety to a place of tranquility. Now I recognize that it's all a matter of training my mind to let go of fear and thus let go of anxiety. In the beginning, my mother's mental illness and my father's abusive alcoholism caused me to feel the gripping pain of anxiety; my stomach was often tied in knots. I developed a fear of the unknown and of the future by worrying about what could happen. What could happen if my mother became ill, if my father came home drunk, if we had to move? The thinking was always about dreadful things that could happen. During the times I lived with my grandparents or aunts and uncles, the anxiety subsided for a short time. Those were short periods of peace and tranquility. Those were times I was genuinely happy as a child because I could really be a child. A child without the worry of adult problems. I didn't have to worry about having enough to eat. I didn't have to feel less important because of where I lived and what I wore.

I still occasionally feel anxiety creep in, but now I recognize what is happening and can usually stop it before it grips my body and causes sleepless nights, upset stomachs, and shallow breathing. I felt this gripping anxiety when I was married to Ulysses and experienced the effects of his outbursts of anger, drunken and controlling behavior and when I was waffling back and forth with my decision to leave him. When I was dating Rick and he would ask me to marry him, the anxiety came flooding in. It was so incredibly stifling that I just wanted to run away. In a sense this is what I did. When I was married to Tom his bullying and badgering caused me anxiety and sadness. I eventually realized he really didn't love me. Not the kind of love a marriage should be based on and that caused me great sadness and anxiety.

It's been a lifetime of work, including counseling, many self-help books, internal healing and understanding and plain growth. When my heart feels one way, and my head feels another, and my stomach is in knots, I am in conflict, and that conflict causes me to go into extreme anxiety. I regress and emotionally, I am again that frightened little girl wondering who will take care of me. During these times I will reflect on what Mayme LaVoy said to me when I was in high school. "You are not like everyone, and don't you forget it." I reflect on what the artist, John Avendano said to me own afternoon when we took a break from working on marketing and were just talking. "Anything bad that can happen has already happened." I remember when my cousin JR once said to me, "You are the bravest person I know." These are the positive thoughts I hold on to and keep, and I let the negative thoughts just come and go.

Too many people in my life have passed away, relatives, friends and acquaintances. Sometimes it's hard to believe that I am so healthy and feel young even though I am now seventy-two. When my father passed away, I had him cremated and the ashes sent to me. He had $1,000 in his savings account and I had them send the funds to me as well. I sent my sister half of the money. She drove up to Washington so we could give him a small ceremony with just the two of us. Sis wrote a poem and read it aloud; I said a few words, and we threw his ashes into the water. I felt sad for him at the time. He was his own worst enemy and died at a young age. He was not a good father to us, and he was not a good husband to our mother. He was a very unhappy man who died alone.

When my mother passed away, she had already paid for her burial at the Veterans home where she lived, so I made sure she had a beautiful ceremony. She developed pancreatic cancer and went quickly. The last time I saw her was on the Fourth of July. I had plans to attend a party, but I kept thinking of Mom all day. I called my very dear friend, Tia, who was going out with me that evening and told her I had to see my mom one more time because I had a feeling she was going to die sometime that night. Tia canceled her plans and drove me to Retsil. Mom was unconscious, but I gave her a kiss and said goodbye to her. She passed away in the night. I am so grateful to Tia for spending that time with me and for providing all the beautiful flowers at my mother's funeral. I felt sad for my mother but was extremely glad I could spend the last few years really getting to know her. One time when I visited her in the hospital, she began to cry. She was unhappy because she said she had no money to leave me. She had given it all to my sister throughout the years. My sister would call quite often and ask for money. I told her I didn't need her money. I said, "Mom, you are the strongest person I know. All you ever wanted was to take care of your two little girls, which you did even while enduring an unhappy marriage with an alcoholic and abusive husband, years of mental illness, and a lifetime of being poor. I thank you for all that you have given me." She stopped crying and touched my hand when I said, "I love you, Mom." It was not until several years later when I was going through a box of her personal affects that I found her will. I didn't even know that she had one. In her will, she wrote, "I leave my entire estate to my daughter, Gloria." Now I understand why she was so upset that day in the hospital. I found my mother's address book and sent her two brothers and three sisters' pictures of the funeral. I also sent a package to my sister, but I never mentioned the will.

When Ulysses died, I helped Crystal and Marcellus plan his funeral. I spoke at the funeral because I wanted our children to know there had been good moments in our marriage and that their father loved them very much. I found saying goodbye to someone at a funeral was a positive way of experiencing closure. After that, I spoke at their grandmother's funeral and their aunt's funeral. I even spoke at Tom and Jamie's funeral. So many people in my life have died.

My cousin JR passed away last year from circumstances stemming from Covid-19. We were more like siblings. We developed a close bond when we were children, and it only grew over the years. We shared so many challenging times and fun times together. He told me once that he wanted his parents to adopt me when I was a little girl. When he told me that I was the bravest person he had ever known, I was so touched hearing this from a man who had spent time in Vietnam and had seen more bravery than what I thought I had ever shown. I was so happy I was able to speak to him on the phone the day before he passed away. Speaking at his funeral did help me put closure on his death. I will always miss him. As I write the last few words of my story,

I find myself reflecting on moments of my past. I am not the same today as I was on that frightening day I looked out the back window of the car to watch the fire burn all our possessions. I no longer worry about who will take care of me, as I have done a fantastic job by myself, with the help of relatives and friends. I am still close to my two friends from childhood, Marge and Sharlene. They are a part of my family. Yes, anxiety does creep in once in a while; however, I am able to keep it at bay. I continue to work on not allowing other people's unhappiness to affect my happiness. This is not easy, especially when it comes to my adult children. Once a parent, always a parent. I feel others' pain so deeply that I am drawn into wanting to solve their problems to make things better for them, and in doing this, I carry their pain. I sometimes get so lost in their feelings that I forget about mine. Something I will always have to work on.

My "empathy" trigger is very strong and deep, and I constantly work to keep it in check. I remember reading that, "Once you've suffered, you don't want anyone else to suffer." That is so true and tells me much about my behavior.

I am learning to live in the moment yet plan for the future, so I do not worry about "What can happen." I know I will end up in a good place. A place better than where I was before. I'm looking forward to years of happiness and peacefulness. There are always peaks and valleys in life, but that's normal. I take one problem at a time and work to make things better or learn to accept what I can't change. I no longer dwell on the past or worry about the future. Anything bad that can happen to me has already happened. I can take chances and not be afraid of turning into a pillar of stone.

My two precious adult children and me; Crystal and Marcellus

Life is Good at 67 (2016

Artist

# John Andro Avendaño

The Art on the front is by the artist John Andro Avendano. It is part of his "Reflection Series" and this piece is called *"The Glance."*

John was born into an artistic family in Arleta, California in 1959. His Mother painted and his brothers drew, and so from an early age he has been a focused artist. He did not settle on just one artistic medium but developed many forms of expressing art by always doing something, always looking for something better than himself, and ever-changing.

John now lives in Washington near his daughter. John shares his studio with his new partner, and they spend most days creating and painting. When not in his Studio, John likes spending time in the Olympic National Forest along the coast of Washington. John puts a new perspective to "plein air" when you view and are inspired by the organic shapes in his paintings. In the near future, John will travel to Spain and walk along the Camino de Santiago and plans to paint along the way. Again, pushing himself both physically, mentally, and spiritually as an Artist.

You can visit John's website to view more of his work at Johnandroavendano.art or sent him an email at john@310@gmail.com

www.ingramcontent.com/pod-product-compliance
Lightning Source LLC
Chambersburg PA
CBHW061648120626
46550CB00003B/864